A
CELEBRATION
OF
MARRIAGE

To Ken and Ellen
From Mom and Dad

With all God's
blessings from the
Author (and your Tutor
in juggling)

Alan S. Green

A
CELEBRATION
OF
MARRIAGE

When Faith Serves Love

RABBI ALAN S. GREEN

ILLUSTRATIONS BY JEAN TETALMAN

Collier Books

Macmillan Publishing Company

New York

Collier Macmillan Publishers

London

Macmillan Publishing Company
866 Third Avenue, New York, N.Y. 10022
Collier Macmillan Canada, Inc.

Library of Congress Cataloging-in-Publication Data
Green, Alan Singer, 1907–
A celebration of marriage.
"Originally published in 1979 as Sex, God, and the
Sabbath—the mystery of Jewish marriage"—T.p. verso.
Bibliography: p.
1. Sex—Religious aspects—Judaism.   2. Marriage—
Religious aspects—Judaism.   I. Green, Alan Singer,
1907–   . Sex, God, and the Sabbath.   II. Title.
BM720.S4G73   1987   296.3'878358   86-24458
ISBN 0-02-095830-7

Macmillan books are available at special discounts for bulk purchases
for sales promotions, premiums, fund-raising, or educational use.
For details, contact:

Special Sales Director
Macmillan Publishing Company
866 Third Avenue
New York, N.Y. 10022

10 9 8 7 6 5 4 3 2 1

Designed by Jack Meserole

Printed in the United States of America

In Tribute
to Frances
My Magnificent Partner
Whose Love
Led Me to Know
the Grand Design

CONTENTS

ACKNOWLEDGMENTS

The author wishes to express his appreciation to his many colleagues for their warm encouragement in the publication of this volume. He is especially grateful for helpful suggestions made to him by Professor Zvi A. Yehuda of the Cleveland College of Jewish Studies and by Professor Lawrence A. Hoffman of the Hebrew Union College–Jewish Institute of Religion, as well as by Morris N. Kertzer, Jerome D. Folkman and Herbert Weiner.

He is happy to acknowledge the unique contribution of Jean Tetalman, whose genius touched these pages with artistry, and the unfailing helpfulness of his secretary, Eva Solomon.

Gratitude is due the following publishers who granted permission to quote passages from their books, specific reference to which is made in the notes: W.W. Norton and Company, Inc.; Pantheon Books, a Division of Random House, Inc.; Little, Brown and Company; Harper & Row, Inc.; Ktav Publishing House, Inc.; Farrar, Straus & Giroux, Inc.; Liveright Publishing Co.; Epworth Press, London; J.P. Tarcher, Inc.

Thinking back, the author recalls fondly and appreciatively the many couples that he counseled before marriage, for they provided the challenge to develop the framework of the concepts presented here; and some responded: "It's beautiful. Why don't you write it?"

INTRODUCTION

"I don't know whether I want to get married. Most of my friends are married and divorced already." These words by my son, then in his late twenties, disturbed me. I knew that his troubled sentiment was shared by many.

Men and women are getting married in no less numbers. But many are entering the new relationship haunted by the sense of the problematic. They miss the feeling of destiny and the conviction that this will be life's grand fulfillment that exalted and excited us in former generations.

Where are the role models that can answer my son's doubts and can show the way? The models are there. All about us there are marriages that are truly secure, with enduring rewards and delights. Most are quiet and hidden. And the attitudes that have gone into them, the philosophy and traditions that make them work, may be even more quiet and hidden. Often they cannot be deeply articulated even by those who hold them. This makes it hard to transmit them effectively to one's children.

This book is written therefore to make clear and moving a vision of life which can lead marriage to its full estate, and which can help a couple to accept and transcend its many problems. It is written for youth who dream of happiness in love and already are formulating attitudes that can make it flower. It is for all who in a radically unsettled world seek the home's classic gift of security.

The Jewish family has been widely acclaimed for its long history of stability and fulfillment. Its strength over a hundred generations has been a decisive factor in Jewish survival. Jewish sages never ceased to plumb the implications of marriage. Their genius made the home a center of faith and observance no less than the synagogue. And the profoundest among them perceived in the love life of man and woman a revelation of the closeness that binds humankind and the Creator. Their illuminations and mystique can help us today.

Young people, especially, hunger for these deeper meanings. They see our society as crowded with externals, afflicted with facelessness and alienation. They are searching for authenticity, genuine inward relationships, and a sense of being attuned to nature and to the ultimate purposes of existence.

The proof of these inner yearnings is seen in the appeal of the various cults of our day. But young men and women who comprehend the rich basis of their biblical faith need not go into strange fields. For the Hebrew bible and idiom provide mystic depths and joyous, life-giving answers.

The classical fountainheads of our religion have sought to foster immediacy and radiance: "With every breath that I breathe, I will praise the Lord" (Psalm 150:1). How can we recapture this spirit? One avenue is surely by understanding in all its profundity the relationship potential of man and woman.

We can begin by considering the innate enthusiasm of children and their delighted communion with all creation. We can study how these sensibilities are diminished, and then ask how we might regain them, maturely and for good.

Before we do so, let me indicate that the convictions of this volume have grown out of a blend of Jewish tradition and personal experience. They are rooted in biblical and rabbinic teachings; and they have been lived through and proved true in the life of the author.

This does not mean that I and my family could dwell perpetually on the high plane of marriage's ideal meaning here described. There were low points, too, as must be expected. But the identification with these teachings helped, and the vision of this goal drew us powerfully toward its realization. My purpose here is to make this goal so luminous that it will exalt us in the best of times, and light a direction even through the inevitable days of darkness and strain.

In the midst of the writing, my beloved companion, Frances, passed away in the forty-third year of our marriage. Some of my congregants and colleagues wrote that our relationship had been an inspiration to them. I hope that these ideas and experiences can touch others.

"Why not open the doors of your beautiful book, *Sex, God and the Sabbath,* and invite the whole community into its search and sentiments?" This challenge from Macmillan Publishing Company set me on an intriguing adventure. It involved little strain since the backgrounds in the Hebrew bible to which I had referred were the original roots for Christian marriage as well as Jewish, and the problems we confront with the surging changes in attitudes toward man and woman, toward "freedom," love, and sex, we all face together.

The newly enlarged book seeks to help us learn more from one another. It searches for explicit ways of applying suggestions made from the Jewish context to marriage in general. It finds new movements in Christian family education that can lend encouragement to parallel efforts in Judaism. And even where parallels are not drawn, it is good for all to know the specific attitudes and observances which have made the Jewish family an example long admired by its neighbors.

We have also included in this edition some updatings of the text which deal with new trends that have emerged since the first writing. For is not our theme, after all, a wrestling of the eternal with the everchanging?

Let me conclude with my deep appreciation for the cheerful encouragement and incisive suggestions given me by Michelle Rapkin, Director, Religious Books, Collier Books/Macmillan Publishing Company.

—ALAN S. GREEN

I

Sex as Design

There are three things too wonderful for me, yea four:
The way of an eagle in the air,
The way of a serpent upon a rock,
The way of a ship in the midst of the sea,
The way of a man with a maid.

—Proverbs 30:18–19

SEX AS DESIGN

Male and female He created them,
and He blessed them,
and He called their name Adam.
—Genesis 5:2

HUMAN EXPERIENCE can take place on many
levels and have many meanings simultane-
ously. The story is told that a sage, observing
the construction of a famous church in Europe, asked
the workmen: "What are you doing?" One replied: "I'm
earning a living." A second answered: "I'm doing my
job, I'm a bricklayer." But a third said: "I'm building a
great cathedral." His sense of participating in a high
purpose beyond himself gave zest to his work and wings
to his spirit.

There is a direction and a lift that can buoy one's
whole life when he or she feels part of a Grand Design,
however we define it. Once we sense this Design, or
even a hint of it, we have confidence that our purposes

will be fulfilled, that our strivings make a difference.

Most of us have deep intimations of a Grand Design from childhood. We are told by our parents that God makes it rain so that the trees and crops can grow and we may have fruit and bread to eat; and that He gives us mothers and fathers to care for us. It is obvious to us then that there is a God: we see the rain and eat the apples and feel the comfort and healing of dear ones. It is a world of wonder and excitement, and we are part of it. The poems of childhood soar with this glory.

But as we grow older, too often the vision is obscured. Most of us live apart from the constant communion with nature. We may no longer perceive rain as the work of God, as the Psalmist did: "You water the mountains from Your upper chambers" (Psalm 104:13). Rather it is heralded by our favorite weather announcer. Or if we think more deeply, it is in a scientific vein: rain comes because it is the nature of water to evaporate from the earth's surface, then to condense in the higher, cooler atmosphere, where it is blown about by the winds caused by the spinning of the earth on its axis. A fascination with science rivets our attention on the "how" of things. We forget about the "why," or, "by what design or intelligence were earth and water so fashioned as to have these characteristics without which our life would be impossible?"

Or we confront cancer and Hitler and violence and slums, and we wonder: "Where is the God of goodness and order amid these things?"

Then we fall in love. From the moment that it happens we know that we are changed. We begin to be lit up with radiance, well-being, and confidence. And if we have been guided—either by others or by our own intuition—to look upon love in its full dimension, the radiance does not dim, but becomes brighter and more pervasive. We marry and commit our lives to care for and comfort another being, and to search for meaning together. We become one in the house in which we dwell, one in the plans by which we live. And, through our basic "male and female" nature, we become one in that ecstatic union of body and mind and soul that is experienced by two who are completely and maturely in love.

The profundity of the sexual union is beautifully implied in the language of the Hebrew Bible. We read that Adam "knew" Eve, his wife (Genesis 4:1). This Hebrew usage teaches that true sexual love involves understanding and communing with another whole person, with another's hopes, talents, insights, as well as with his or her body and feelings. In the very strokes of love one finds himself or herself expressing acceptance, appreciation, adoration.

Indeed, one is amazed by the way in which the physical sensations are transmuted and absorbed by the communion of spirits, and the self is forgotten in the exaltation of and concern for the beloved. The Scriptures put it: "Therefore shall a man leave his father and his mother and cleave to his wife, and they shall become one flesh" (Genesis 2:24). This implies a seamless unity of body and spirit.

One is immediately struck by the profundity with which the biblical accounts approach sex and demonstrate awareness of its full implications, especially in contrast with some of the modern attitudes. Professor Alfred Kinsey, concentrating on its physiological aspects, calls sex experience an "outlet," connoting a release from the emotional compulsions and glandular pressures by which man is driven. Judaism, regarding it in a wider context, considers the marital union rather an "insight," a self-directed avenue of one's search for meaning.

Here we turn to the writings of one of the most influential authorities of the Middle Ages, Nachmanides (Rabbi Moses ben Nachman, 1194–1270), who was deeply concerned with our theme. As a Talmudist, biblical commentator, and communal leader, he was involved in restoring emotion and mystery in Judaism, as a counterbalance to the stress on rational philosophy by the great Maimonides (Rabbi Moses ben Maimon, 1135–1204) before him. It is interesting that both of these figures of the Spanish period were students of the human body, for by profession they were physicians.

An elaborate letter, attributed to Nachmanides, instructs a friend on the profound meaning and proper procedure of marital union. It is called "Iggeret Ha-Kodesh," meaning "Epistle on Holiness," for it equates that union with holiness. Although scholars today question its authorship, its association with Nachmanides's name, as well as its moving phrases, have led it to become a cherished and widely quoted writing. Here it elaborates on the biblical terminology:

Know that the sexual intercourse of man with his wife is holy and pure when done properly, in the proper time and with the proper intention. Proper sexual intercourse is called "knowing." Unless it involved matters of great holiness, it would not be called "knowing."

And it goes on to stress the central role of *knowledge* in the Jewish faith and in the Divine economy.

More recent counselors have been returning to a perspective closer to the biblical concept. Masters and Johnson, authorities in the field of sexual adjustment, emphasize throughout their book, *The Pleasure Bond*, that there can be no enduring sex fulfillment without a growing, insightful relationship between two total personalities.

As the union develops through loving and sharing, each partner is suffused more and more with a sense of Design: how a man is designed for a woman, and a woman for a man—physically and spiritually. We observe that neither can be complete or fulfilled without the other, and that life itself could not be continued without this pattern. We know that we did not create it. It was here long before we were.

The conviction grows that the man-woman design is so complex, so fantastic that it can hardly be the result of an accident. Surely it must reflect some intelligence at work; it must speak to us of the Designer. And we sense that it is so rewarding and sustaining, with a warmth that permeates our whole existence, that it must be the gift of One who cares for man and seeks his good.

Searching on, the couple comes to appreciate that this powerful attraction, this strangely compounded charge of electricity, chemistry, and psychology that brings them together, is not an isolated force just for them, or even for the human race. Rather it is a fundamental element of all creation: the emotive thrust of life itself.

Indeed, what would creation be without life? What would the whirling suns, the mountains, seas, and streams signify if there were no living creatures to perceive and appreciate them? Surely a high point in the whole design came when the Designer somehow recombined the dull, dreamless atoms of stone and sea and air and perhaps a spark of sunlight to fashion living creatures. And from the moment when life was born, He put within it this drive to continue life, that it might become ever more developed and sentient and able to search out and ponder the world before it. This drive to reproduce, which began with simple fission, early evolved into male and female forms whose partnership was needed for the very flower, the very ant to endure. This is the principle that pervades all but the most rudimentary creatures and sparks the drive to mate, to unite for the sake of life itself.

Sex, the man-womanness that we experience so profoundly, is thus basic to creation itself. It is not an incident, or a trimming, or a mere private pleasure. It is intrinsic, indispensable to the Grand Design. Indeed, it is the revelation of that Design to us in a most intimate, persuasive, and powerful way.

Couples are coming more and more to look upon childbirth as a profound shared experience, bringing them insights of purpose and wonder. They are rejecting a pattern that long made it almost entirely a physical and medical matter. Here hygienic perfection and the "relief of pain"—often with the semianesthetizing of the mother—blotted out all other considerations. Instead many parents are seeking natural childbirth, in which the mother can be fully alert and conscious of the depth of the imponderable moment.

They are thinking in terms of "bonding," which has come to describe the linking of sights and warmth and affection and souls between mother and child, and indeed between father and child, in his or her first minutes of independent life. They are rejecting the snatching away of the baby into some antiseptic, isolated loneliness. And they are seeking the "bonding" that occurs between participating husband and wife through the whole experience, deepening their awareness of their unique, ineffable, cosmic roles together.

True lovers thus come to an abiding conviction that there is a plan, an order, in this world. "There is a God," if you like to put it, as I do, in the way that people have expressed it for so long. But it makes little difference how you state it. For there are many creeds, and many ways to point to this sense of Order, or Intelligence. (And all confess that human terminology is inadequate to define or encompass an Intelligence which is on a level so much above ours.) What is important is that we perceive that here, through our love, we have gone beyond our own little lives and have shared in a spectacular way in the very process of creation.

There are many evidences that we live in a realm that transcends our own volition: our very birth is one. But we are not "all there" to experience it. The events of love, however, reveal that plan with a poignancy.

Our physical maturity comes upon us without our promotion. We "fall in love" sometimes when we scarcely intend to. Above all, the love act itself gives marvelous evidence of the blend of our will and the Grand Will. It is our own decision to begin to make love to our mate, but then we are swept along by a flood of physiological and emotional tides which are properly beyond our volition. We have become part of the Beyond, unforgettably.

Professor Alan Watts, a psychologist and religionist of our day, writes in his moving *Nature, Man and Woman*:

The full splendor of sexual experience does not reveal itself without a new mode of attention to the world in general. . . . It is [not only] the most dramatic instance of union between oneself and the other, . . . but a special mode or degree of the total intercourse of man and nature. Its delight is an intimation of the ordinarily repressed delight which inheres in life itself, in our fundamental but normally unrealized identity with the world.

He suggests that the laughter that often follows spontaneously in the wake of such intimacy should be greeted as an echo and intimation of the essential joy that pervades the world. Indeed, Dante described the song of the angels as "the laughter of the universe." And Professor Watts concludes: "Sexuality is not a separate compartment of human life, it is a radiance pervading every human relationship."

The radiance is there, with all its warmth and security, because it is lit by the sense that we are part of an Order, good and enduring. This does not mean that we have solved the problems that confound us: Why cancer, holocaust, violence? But it does mean that we have built up so much faith and insight that our spiritual reservoir will still have reserves despite the heavy drains that the world's evils may make upon it. Indeed, our love keeps replenishing that reservoir.

II

Sex as Revelation

No man without woman,
No woman without man,
No couple without God.
—Midrash, Genesis
Rabba 22:2

SEX AS REVELATION

For love is strong as death,
Its flashes are flashes of fire,
A very flame of the Lord.
— Song of Songs 8:6

SEXUALITY is a revelation of God and of His plan. This is a recurrent melody in the symphony of Jewish teaching from its beginning. The first chapters of Genesis were meant to inspire man to marvel at and be grateful for creation. Therefore its most striking elements were singled out: "Let there be *light*, and there was light!" (Who can be unresponsive to the lift of light?) "And the earth brought forth . . . tree bearing fruit, wherein is the seed thereof, *after its kind*." (The tiny seed holds the exact blueprint for the new creation!) "And God created man in His own image, *male and female* He created them." (The man-womanness of our life is to be regarded as among the primary and most pervasive of wonders.)

The Rabbis made a striking comment on this creation story. They referred to the terms "good impulse" and "evil impulse" (Yetzer Tov veYetzer HaRa), which popular parlance used to describe the motivations of human beings. The "good impulse" was connected with their charitable, unselfish tendencies. The "evil impulse" was associated with their instinctive drives, especially sex, which can be selfish. The Rabbis said that when God saw the completion of creation, and said, "Behold it is very good" (Genesis 1:31), the word "good" refers to the good impulse. But the word "very" refers to the Yetzer HaRa, the so-called but not really "evil" impulse, that is, the sex impulse. "For without it," said our ancient teachers, "a man would not build a house, marry a wife, beget children and labor for their support."

The very first command of God to humankind, they stressed, comes in these same opening sentences of the Torah: "Be fruitful and multiply and replenish the earth" (Genesis 1:28). The various Rabbis constantly emphasized marriage as the fulfillment of both the Divine plan and the human need. They elaborated on the Torah's concept: "It is not good that a man should be alone" (Genesis 2:18), and said: "The unmarried live without joy, without blessing, without good. . . . Without Torah, without a protecting wall . . . without peace."

"No man without woman, no woman without man, no couple without God," is the way the Rabbis summed it up.

It must be pointed out that these comments cannot be taken narrowly. Their purpose was not a negative one; they were not meant to imply that a single person cannot live a spiritual life or gain insight into God's great plan. The statements were rather directed positively: to encourage marriage and depict how it can facilitate spiritual growth.

It was said among the mystics of our people that God loves man and woman with a tenderness and a longing that they cannot grasp, but that they can get an inkling of it in one's tenderness and longing for one's mate.

The most dramatic evidence of the Jewish doctrine that sex should be an avenue to God is a Talmudic injunction, first given to scholars and then applied to the whole house of Israel. It is that the Sabbath should be enhanced by human love, and that on it therefore a man and his wife should join in sexual union.

Why the Sabbath? Because the Sabbath is the day of God, the day of completion, of wholeness and peace. All three of these meanings are contained in the word Shalom, which we use in the greeting of this day: Shabbat Shalom. And husband and wife are complete and at peace when they are united in true love with each other and with their God. Shabbat (which is the Hebrew way of pronouncing it) is a "foretaste of paradise," said the Rabbis. How fitting for the ecstatic experience!

A holy act should be performed on a holy day. Such is the implication of the letter attributed to Nachmanides. And together with his fellow mystics he related it to their overarching doctrine of "Yihud," or the supreme Unity of things below and above, which we shall discuss later.

III

Pleasure as a Gift
of God

Blessed be the Lord,
Who causes the bridegroom
to rejoice with the bride.
— from the Hebrew wedding
ceremony

PLEASURE AS A GIFT
OF GOD

How precious is Your kindness, O God,
You make the children of men
To drink out of the fountain of Your pleasures.
                              —Psalm 36:8–9

The False Division into Body and Soul

SOME MAY FIND strange this portrayal of our sexuality as a special token of the Divine spark within us. That is because we in the western tradition have been accustomed to think of the human being as composed of two parts, the body and the soul. And we have associated the body with the lower, inferior, common aspects of our being. We may think: Surely then it is not through the body that one comes to the sense of the Holy One!

The Greek philosopher, Plato, crystalized this dichotomy in his distinction between matter and form. Forms (concepts of the mind) he declared to be perfect and eternal. But matter (the actual physical thing before us) is imperfect. It is subject to "generation and decay," to formation and dissolution, birth and death, and its existence is limited. Thus the "form" or blueprint or concept of a chair is perfect, and endures forever. But any actual chair that you see, composed of wood and nails et cetera, is bound to have certain imperfections, and also it must ultimately wear out.

According to this thinking, the "form" of man is his soul. It is beautiful and perfect and destined for life eternal. The trouble is that it must be joined to a body to produce the actual man or woman. The body has imperfections: it is subject to illness, deterioration, and death, and it pulls the soul away from the ideal life by its selfish hungers and lusts. Therefore many faiths have insisted that to be a spiritual person one has to subdue, deny, "mortify" the body.

Thus the delight of food has been considered by some a mortal danger since it can lead to gluttony and to such excesses as the notorious banquets of ancient Rome. The pious Buddhist monk is given a begging bowl into which well-wishers can place a bit of rice, just enough to sustain his life.

Alcoholic beverages have been prohibited by many religions. For do they not open the door to drunkenness, vulgarity and violence!

Sex has been looked down upon and rejected by some ascetic interpretations of religion which insist that man must give up this tremendous impulsion of the

senses and remain celibate if he is to attain the highest
level of purity and spirituality.

Judaism's Sanctification of Pleasure

Judaism differs from all of these. It stresses the oneness of the human being. The body and the soul work
together. Both are created by God. Both are equally
beautiful. Each affords insights into God's ways. There
is nothing vulgar, nothing "carnal" about bodily delights.

On the contrary, the pleasures of this world are
given to man as a sign of God's goodness. They reveal
His nearness and His care. They are for us to enjoy.
The Talmud Yerushalmi declares: "Man will have to
render account [to God] for all the good things which
his eyes beheld but which he refused to enjoy."

Only we must be sure that we *use these pleasures in
a proper way*, in a way that pleases both mankind and
the Creator who designed them. Then they will be
avenues to insight, expanding the spirit. Thus employed they will avoid the dangers of indulgence, in-
temperance, and sensuality.

So it is that the Jew is enjoined to eat, and to eat
in accordance with the full demands of health. He is
to direct the savor of the food to enlarge his enjoyment
and with it his gratefulness to God, the giver of the
food. The ancient triple command of the Torah is:
"VeAchalta, veSavata, uVerachta—You shall eat, and
be satisfied, and bless [the Lord your God for the good

land He has given you]" (Deuteronomy 8:10). This was taken up by the Rabbis and included in the Bircat haMazon—the blessing that is traditionally sung after every meal "for the land and for the food." The remarkable word is Savata—be satisfied, have plenty. Jewish observance encourages abundant and especially delectable food for each festival. The Rabbis said that one should borrow from the other days of the week to enhance his Sabbath meal as a bountiful symbol of God's goodness.

Wine is used in virtually every Jewish ceremony. We raise the cup and bless God for having "created the fruit of the vine," which the Psalmist tells us He did "to gladden the heart of man" (Psalm 104:15). Thus wine, far from being an evil, can encourage man to come closer to God, to appreciate His goodness, and to "serve Him with gladness" (Psalm 100:2).

It is customary to put the wine into a special goblet, a Kiddush Cup, literally a Cup of Holiness. This can be for us an instructive symbol of Judaism's approach to pleasure: Enjoy it. But receive it understandingly. Put it into a *sacred setting*, where it belongs. *Pour it as it were into a Kiddush Cup.*

It is interesting to learn that this usage of wine in a holy way turns man away from indulging in an excessive, destructive manner. For here, contrary to ordinary drinking, one seeks not to gratify oneself but to extol God, not to get "high" but to sense the Most High, not to escape from the world but to comprehend it more profoundly. A study done at Yale University revealed that groups that regularly employ wine for sacramental purposes rarely succumb to alcoholism. Indeed, the Jewish folk has been historically noted for its freedom from drunkenness.

It is in the same pattern that sex is welcomed as among the richest of all God's gifts. It, too, is to be set in a spiritual framework, namely marriage. The very ceremony of the Jewish wedding is called "Kiddushin," or "Sanctification." And the blessings involved combine the sense of pleasure and the sense of sacredness so completely that you cannot tell where one leaves off and where the other begins. The central "Sheva Berachot" ("Seven Blessings") extol God for "creating everything for Your glory," for "fashioning man in Your image," for "creating joy and gladness, bridegroom and bride, mirth and exaltation, pleasure and delight, love and harmony, peace and companionship . . . Blessed are You, who cause the bridegroom to rejoice with the bride."

We should note that some Jewish sects did indeed extol celibacy. During the generations of suffering under Roman persecution there was bitter dissension and recrimination among the various parties. The Essenes and the men of Qumran (site of the Dead Sea Scrolls) withdrew from what they considered the defilement of everyday life and the corruption of the cities and the Temple. They formed "purified" monastic communities that emphasized ritual cleanliness, communal baptism, and communal meals.

John the Baptist, who lived and preached and baptized beside the Jordan River, only miles from them, may have been touched by their teachings. Whether or not these influenced Paul and early Christianity is not clear. We do know that Paul discouraged marriage:

I say therefore to the unmarried and the widows, it is good that they abide even as I [unmarried]. But if they cannot contain, let them marry. . . . He who marries does well; but he who refrains from marriage does better (I Corinthians 7:8–9, 38).

Today the Catholic Church's doctrine demands of its highest religious leaders that they abstain from sex. Priests are to lead celibate lives. Nuns are to elevate their feelings by being "married spiritually" to Jesus.

Normative Judaism has always rejected excursions into asceticism. Indeed, one of its most remarkable and persuasive aspects has been its naturalism. It refuses to consider pleasure an enemy of faith. Instead, by plumbing its significance and sanctifying its use, Judaism has turned pleasure into a powerful ally of religion and the life fulfilled.

An English scholar, David Mace, writes in his book, *Hebrew Marriage*:

I would like to comment on the notable absence in the Old Testament of any kind of sexual asceticism. The entirely positive attitude to sex which the Hebrews adopted was to me an unexpected discovery. It is true that I had always been struck by the unembarrassed plainness of speech with which they discussed sexual matters. But I had not fully realized that it had the roots in an essentially "clean" conception of the essential goodness of the sexual function. This is something very difficult for us to grasp, reared as we have been in a tradition which has produced in many minds the rooted idea that sex is essentially sinful. That sex can be a gift of God, to be received with gratitude and enjoyed freely, is a truth too long forgotten, and sorely in need of revival.

It is significant in this connexion that there should be no apparent sign in the Old Testament of those psycho-sexual disorders which abound in our time. I can recall no reference to male impotence, and the Hebrew wife seemed to enjoy unashamedly her sex relationship with her husband. It is a great pity that the inhibited Christian mind has obscured for us all too often those wholesome features of Old Testament marriage.

The letter attributed to the thirteenth-century rabbinic teacher, Nachmanides, to which we have referred, and which in any case may well reflect his view, expresses great distress that such negative attitudes had come in to afflict Jewish minds:

No one should think that sexual intercourse is ugly and loathsome. God forbid! The matter is not as Rabbi Moses (Maimonides) of blessed memory said in his *Guide to the Perplexed*. He was incorrect in praising Aristotle for stating that the sense of touch is shameful for us. Heaven forbid! . . . For if sexual intercourse was repulsive, then the reproductive organs are also repulsive. . . . But everything created with divine wisdom is complete, exalted, good, and pleasant. But when man sins, ugliness becomes attached to these matters, as they were not repulsive or abhorrent originally. Understand this well.

It is fascinating to observe how Judaism used the power of love to energize and enrich religious devotion. Let us look at portions of the Song of Songs, a biblical book of unabashed love poems from quite ancient times. The very fact that it was accepted into the Holy Scriptures testifies to the naturalness, the absence of prudery, in classic Judaism. And the fact that these verses were then used in worship makes them all the more striking:

> The song of songs, which is Solomon's.
> Let him kiss me with the kisses of his mouth
> > For your love is better than wine. . . .
> My beloved is unto me as a bag of myrrh
> > That lies between my breasts. . . .
> I am come into my garden. . . .
> > I am my beloved's and my beloved is mine. . . .
> My beloved is white and ruddy,
> > His locks are curled.
> His body is as polished ivory,
> > His legs are as pillars of marble. . . .
> How beautiful are your steps in sandals,
> > O prince's daughter!
> The roundings of your thighs are like the links of a chain.
> > Your naval is like a round goblet. . . .
> > Your breasts are like two fauns, twins of a gazelle. . . .
> > Set me as a seal upon your heart,
> For love is strong as death.
> > Its flashes are flashes of fire,
> A very flame of the Lord.

These are some of the passionate phrases of the book which traditionally is chanted in its entirety before the service of welcoming the Sabbath. The concepts are mentally directed to the Holy One. For according to rabbinic tradition, King Solomon in the story represents God, the husband, and the Shulamite is Israel, His bride; and the tale is an allegory of the love that binds them fast to each other. Rabbi Akiva, who was martyred at the time of the Bar Kochba revolt, about 135 C.E., affirmed that "all the Writings [the Ketuvim, or last section of the Bible] are holy, but the Song of Songs is holy of holies." Commended by this eminent sage, and well known and cherished by regular Sabbath usage, the expressions of the Song of Songs sealed the profound association in the Jewish mind between holiness and human love. Consider how this association works for beauty both ways: For if the coming before the Lord calls to mind the beloved in sublime form, will not the coming before our beloved call to mind the presence of God?

Throughout the Jewish world the Sabbath is welcomed as a bride. For what is there on earth more lovely and appealing? Therefore the most favored of all opening hymns—to which hundreds of melodies have been composed—is "Lecha Dodee," signifying "Come, beloved":

> Come, beloved, the bride to meet,
> The presence of the Sabbath let us greet.
> —Song of Songs 7:12

The beloved is the people of Israel; the bride is Shabbat.

Many a congregation will dramatize this greeting by turning and facing the entrance doors of the synagogue during this song. This follows the custom of the Kabbalists of Safed during the sixteenth century, in a period in which the mystic Isaac Luria was prominent. Each Friday they would gather on the slopes of the majestic hills to the west of the city, to await the setting of the sun. And as the Sabbath arrived, they would escort the "bride" with song back to their house of worship.

Thus for Judaism the glow of bride and groom is the very symbol—the archetype—of all joy, human and divine.

IV

Reliving the Honeymoon Every Week

Shabbat—A day set apart
to renew the transcendence of our love.

RELIVING THE HONEYMOON
EVERY WEEK

As a man rejoices all the days of the wedding feast,
So does he rejoice on the Sabbath.
As the groom does no work on the day he is wed,
So he does none on Shabbat.
                    —Al Nakawa

Shabbat as a Reliving of the Honeymoon

B UOYANT HEARTS within us sense the wonder of
love as a gift of God. Searching minds, reinforced
by the teachings of sages, come ever more to see
it as an evidence of His nearness. *How then shall we find
the way* to pour out our thankfulness to Him, and to
sustain forever these insights? The answer is: the Sabbath.

For the Jewish people, *the Sabbath evening table is a*

dramatic celebration and exaltation of human love. This is a hidden truth, all too often unrecognized.

We are aware that the Sabbath encompasses many things, that it is the sacred vessel that preserves the very essence of Jewish learning and longing. And many in our age are seeking to recapture the healing serenity and spiritual reaffirmation of this special day.

We are acquainted with the moving, explicit meanings of the ceremonies which usher it in within the sanctuary of our homes: The candle flames are a sign of God's presence, of His guidance to light our path. The wine stands for the delights of life, which He wants us to relish, and to appreciate as evidence of His nearness and His care. The chant that goes with it sings of God's special love and election of Israel. It recalls "the work of creation," after which God "rested on the seventh day . . . and hallowed it" (Genesis 2:2–3). It reminds us of the "deliverance from Egypt," where as slaves we learned firsthand the importance of providing a day of rest to all, including those who labor. It stresses that the Sabbath was the first, and remains primary, among all the holy days. Then the Challa, or twisted loaf, bespeaks the gift of life itself and of the means to sustain it.

But now as a couple, our minds are opened to another dimension, deep within and not referred to by the words: When the wife sets the stage for the Sabbath to come in by blessing the candles, the world stops. The modest rays miraculously vanquish and blot out the harsh glare of tensions and pressures that may surround us. Business, car pools, disappointments, and debts are pushed aside. Fears slink off and disappear. And a husband, looking at his mate—exalted and beauteous in prayer, her eyes sparkling in the flame's reflections—will thank God for her: for her body and her soul, which are now all one to him as her true lover, and for the comfort and completion, the motivation and confidence, which she has brought to him.

Then, as the husband raises the cup of wine and chants the Kiddush prayer with all the tenderness and melody of which he is capable (God grant him a sweet voice!), she looks upon him steadfastly and thanks the Creator for all the strength and sustenance, the promise of children and the future, which he has brought to her. The world which is always threatening to overwhelm and enslave us with its duties, demands, and deadliness—"getting and spending we lay waste our powers," wrote Wordsworth—has now been subdued. The subtler, more tender sentiments have their chance again, and renew within us the intimations of happiness when first we met, the ecstacy of the reward when first we were wed, the purposiveness of all our being together. Shabbat is indeed the celebration of human love in the presence of God who made it His gift as part of His design.

The Sabbath is a reliving of the honeymoon. For what is a honeymoon but the declaration that the world and its pressures must give way to the two of us and our love! We proclaim that our occupations and varied pursuits—crucial, stature nourishing, time consuming as they are—must yet be kept in balance and made to enhance and nurture the ultimate satisfaction of our hearts: "Male and female He created them, and He blessed them, and called their name Adam"(Genesis 5:2).

The Hebrew idiom speaks not of honeymoon, but of Shivat Y'me HaMishteh, or Seven Days of the Wedding Feast, to which reference is made in the quotation at the beginning of this section. We could playfully coalesce the two languages and call it a honeyweek. Then we might say that Shabbat enables us to recapture the wonder, vision, and avowals of the honeyweek weekly!

Around the Shabbat table we reaffirm that God has given us a sacred fire, that we are priest and priestess committed above all to tending it on our (His) altar, and that nothing must be allowed to dim or quench it. Shabbat, with its delicate sensibilities, its mood of peace and completion, its "foretaste of paradise," culminating in its marital intimacy as a special "mitzva" (a good deed enjoined by God himself), is the honeymoon all over again. It is a day to be set apart, to renew and refresh the transcendence of our love. Once we awaken to this, and cherish Shabbat accordingly, it can be an incalculable boon in keeping tenderness alive in the world which seems bent on stripping us of mystery and romance. Let it be so from the first Sabbath of our marriage, that its song and ceremony may capture and forever preserve the radiance and revelation of love's beginning.

Gates of Prayer, the New Union Prayer Book, declares that "Through the centuries, Israel has given itself to the Sabbath, seeing it as the climax of its life, even as it was the climax of creation." We must see it also as the climax of our love, even as it is of creation.

What a gift our forefathers have handed down to us! As children we could scarcely hope to understand all its roles. As adults we can scarcely afford not to.

Many a couple might have triumphed over the strains and differences inevitable in marriage and been spared much unhappiness or even separation had they observed the Sabbath each week, celebrating God and their love as their adventure supreme. The tension of concentrating on what *I* want might well have softened under the influence of what *my mate* wants, what *my marriage* wants, and what *God* wants and offers to me in His plan, during the quiet Sabbath atmosphere.

Sex—God—Sabbath: three concepts, yet see how they are intertwined! They are three aspects of a single reality: life coming into being, and then sustained, through love. Is there any reality closer to us than this? *Keep these joined in your thought and conduct: sex, God, and the Sabbath*, and you will be on your way to the bright purposiveness and to the security that you seek together.

There should be a place in every couple's schedule, sacred and welcomed for each and all of these three. A time for *sex*, when one is unhurried, unharried, and unexhausted. It is amazing that this drive, so insistent, can yet be neglected and shunted aside. The demands of careers and the ambitions of social status tend to monopolize our prime energies, allowing only scraps and leftovers for our life of love. Occasions, therefore, must be deliberately sought to cherish and renew the physical revelation of our bodies, when we are fresh and undistracted. Daytimes, if you choose, as well as night. Little honeymoons, away from home routines, and often closer to the woods and waves of God's creation.

A time for *God*, to search for Him, and to commune with Him in many ways. In the wordless intimations of nature. In the symbols and ceremonies of the sanctuary, eloquent with the memories of one's youth and the youth of one's people. In the evocative concepts of poets and singers. But time must be allotted, for the sense of God does not come instantaneously, as if by computer.

A time for *Shabbat*, whose very strength lies in the fact that it is fixed in time. You do not have to seek it out. It seeks you. There it is, every seventh day. And if you determine that you will greet it, and begin to observe its spoken and unspoken meanings, it will grow and so will its rewards.

The Sabbath provides a clear corrective to a problem that Masters and Johnson cite in *The Pleasure Bond*:

There is a danger of letting everyday chores and responsibilities come between you as husband and wife, so that you are always postponing the pleasure of having each other's company because there is work to be done.

It would probably amaze you to know how many husbands and wives become sexually dysfunctional as a result of the so-called work ethic.

So let there be a Shabbat ethic!

Indeed, cherishing intimacy within the Sabbath setting is highly conducive to its success in many ways:

Physically the couple is rested, having broken away from their outside labors and their household chores (hopefully long before the Sabbath begins), and having refreshed themselves in preparation for the sacred day. The grace and manners about the Sabbath table prepare them with an added measure of tenderness toward each other. Spiritually they are exalted with the sense of the Presence felt so near their family. Little wonder that the special mitzva of love's union on Shabbat became one of the most welcome and well observed of all the commandments.

As our falling in love may have opened our path to a sure sense of God, so the celebration of our love on Shabbat summons us now to the full and many-faceted splendor of this Seventh Day of Delight, in which our being, freed from material concerns and from the tyranny of success and failure, finds true rest and reward amid thoughts and values that are priceless and eternal.

Turning Visions into Realities

Shabbat, with its exalted effects just depicted, is one of Judaism's greatest treasures, a stimulating pattern to learn from, a high point in this book. But for many it is a lost treasure, lost in the hustle of American life, with only perfunctory observance and a minimal grasp of the gifts it can bring. To make it live again in the Jewish people will require all the skill and persuasion that its leaders can muster.

One tends to think of the Christian Sunday, too, as a picture of "former days" when it encompassed not only the church service in the morning and coming home to a festive Sunday dinner, but the reading of the family Bible by the father, the paterfamilias, to wife and children, with the interchange of guidance and blessings, of ideas and experiences that brought together in love all those around the table. With the decline of this tradition, Christian leaders, too, have seen their work cut out for them and have been seeking new techniques to restore these values.

The Marriage Encounter Parallel

The Christian marriage encounter experience has been one of the most ingenious and spectacularly effective of these efforts to restore the spiritual value of the family. A group meets away from home for a weekend. A team of leaders gives a short introduction. They offer themselves as examples. Sharing what the encounter has meant to them personally, they illustrate the techniques of deeper self-search and enhanced communication which each couple is to pursue in the two days ahead. A priest, or a ministerial or rabbinical couple, is always part of the team, not to instruct, but to reveal the enlarged vision of love which came to them through the encounter, and to relate its essence to their religious faith. Then for two days each couple is put in a setting of complete privacy and relaxation. Left utterly together and uninterrupted, they carry forward the suggested methods of written and oral communication that open new dimensions of mutual understanding and of the glory and reward of their affection.

When I first wrote this book it occurred to me that the marriage encounter is really like the Hebrew Sabbath in that each is a "reliving of the honeymoon." Later I was delighted to find almost the very words of this chapter echoed in Father Chuck Gallagher's inspiring volume on the marriage encounter: "It is like a second honeymoon. . . . It brings out the dreams, hopes and ambitions that a couple had when they first fell in love, got engaged and were married."

Indeed, although there are great differences, certain parallels are striking: There is the determined consecration of time, setting aside hours which are inviolate, unharried by the ordinary pressures of career, bills, and social responsibilities of day-to-day life. There is the focus on our love as our possession beyond compare and on the realization that our need is not to have more beauty given to us, but to uncover and sustain the wonder already within us in the potential of that love. There is the assurance of the religious setting, in which we share the wisdom and sacred practices of the generations of yesterday, and the insight that our "little" love is part of God's Grand Design and perfecting it can help Him heal His troubled world for tomorrow.

As faith can serve love, so love can serve faith. Father Gallagher describes eloquently how these celebrations of marriage can revitalize the Christian Church and raise hopes for our advancement toward God's Kingdom.

Participants have come away from the marriage encounter with such enthusiasm that they have felt compelled to bring others in. So the numbers have multiplied; and from its origins in Catholic circles, the program has been adopted and adapted in the Protestant and Jewish communities.

What of those who are touched with no such enthusiasm, who say: "Where there's real love you don't need any ceremonies, or encounters, or Sabbaths; and if that love is not there, these won't create it"?

Love is not a "thing" that we have or don't have. It is a flower that grows out of our whole being. It can be nurtured into ever richer blossoms, or it can be neglected and allowed to fade—sometimes so imperceptibly that we pay it no heed. That's it! It's our heed, our attention that is crucial. We all want—above all else—to love and to be loved, but our attention is swept into a myriad of other channels. *Celebrations are great reminders.* They bring us back. As the Sabbath comes regularly week by week, and we first commit, and then habitutate, ourselves to its renewal, so the marriage encounter provides for a daily dialogue in which each couple refreshes and continues the processes of deeper communication which they learned. In these consecrated moments the husband and wife renew not only their skills but the celebration of their love.

V

Recovering the Home as a Fountain of Faith

More than the Jewish people have kept the Sabbath,
the Sabbath has kept the Jewish people.
—Ahad Ha-am

RECOVERING THE HOME AS A FOUNTAIN OF FAITH

The Jewish Child and the Jewish Future

THE CHILD is the perceptible proof of the Design. He or she is the unmistakable evidence that through our love we have been partners in creation. The child's growth is then the continuously unfolding revelation of blueprints of such intricacy and wisdom that we can but stand in awe. But we don't stand for long. With a child now added to the household, there is too much work to be done. Yet we find the sweep of life's meaning in the very tasks involved in his or her guidance.

Here the Sabbath plays a special role. For if he comes into a home in which Shabbat is observed, then before he can speak a word, he begins to build the spiritual basis for his life. From the ceremonies about the table he absorbs a feeling for the subtle phenomenon called worship. He observes his parents not working or laughing or eating, but expressing a unique mood: reverent, illuminated, addressing a Presence beyond themselves, which he too comes to sense. Long before he can say God, the child gains a feeling for Him.

As his parents bless each other in the ceremonies, and then bless and kiss him, he gains an explicit insight into how much a husband and wife love each other and how that love shelters and nourishes their love for their child. From the songs and phrases, he develops a taste for the beauty and power of the Hebrew language. Soon the Sabbath becomes a special time for parents to read him stories of bible and Israel.

As the Sabbath grows in meaning and joy for the child, his very response encourages the commitment of the parents. We observe this in the increasing reintroduction into Jewish homes of Havdala. This charming ceremony, signifying "separation," ushers out the Sabbath day and divides it from the working week about to begin.

Havdala, held in the dusk-awe of the waning twilight of the Sabbath afternoon, is short in verbalization and rich in unique symbols. Its twisted candle of many leaping flames bespeaks the might and mystery of creation, when God first said: "Let there be light." Its spice box may be fashioned in a variety of forms: a castle tower, a fish, a pear tree. It is passed around for all to savor in order that they may keep the fragrant appeal of this beloved day even beyond its hours. These, plus the more familiar wine and the simple melodies summoning Elijah as the forerunner of the Messiah and then wishing all "A Good Week," make Havdala particularly attractive to the child. He experiences it with the total panoply of his senses: sight, taste, smell, touch, hearing. The family is drawn close by the wonder of Shabbat—beyond words—felt together. "Our children simply insist on this delightful spiritual moment," said a young father to me.

A marriage counselor, Esther Oshiver Fisher, comments on how the Sabbath pattern "welds family and religion together. This faith has given [the child] the feeling of being part of the generations that have come and gone and of those that will be, . . . an awareness of the flow of time. Some day he, as others before, will use those rituals to transmit to his children the wondrous feeling for life that he received from his parents a long time ago."

With this feeling, and with the models of father and mother made dramatic on the Sabbath before him, the child brings with him to synagogue and religious school a fertile soil in which the seeds of instruction and inspiration can take root and flourish. *Without it they cannot.*

Heinrich Heine well portrayed the crucial role of the Jewish home during the dark days of the Middle Ages, as "a haven of rest from the storms that raged round the very gates of the ghettos, nay a fairy palace in which the bespattered objects of the mob's derision threw off their garb of shame and resumed the royal attire of free men."

But will the Jewish people keep that strength in a new world that is open, that is relatively friendly and free, and that no longer forces it to make the home its bastion? Only if it realizes that the Jewish home is still crucial not only to its own happiness and to the welfare of its children, but to the very survival of the Jew. And only if it understands that the Sabbath is still its unique and indispensable instrument.

These two are the central convictions in study after study of the Jewish family and of Jewish survival. Joseph M. Yoffey writes in his introduction to the comprehensive volume produced by the Jewish Marriage Education Council of England:

It is impossible to exaggerate the effect of the Sabbath upon Jewish home life. Week after week all the members of the family, in an atmosphere of physical well-being and spiritual serenity come together and form a single harmonious unit, enjoying one another's company, confiding in each other, learning from each other, and creating an Oneg Shabbat which leaves its imprint upon them throughout life.

We should ask ourselves the question: What is the source of the fantastic contributions of the Jew to the literature, learning, idealism, artistry, and healing of the world? Is it not the remarkable preparation and school achievement of the Jewish child? And what is the source of this? Is it not the strength and sanctity of the Jewish home, and the unbounded investment which Jewish parents make in their children? One cannot fail to be impressed with the tremendous demands and stimuli with which Jewish families surround their offspring. From the earliest months, each word is encouraged, then cherished, remarked, and repeated to others: "My child said this." From nursery school and kindergarten on, attainment is expected, rewarded, and its absence noted and labored over.

What makes the little Jewish child able to endure, and willing to accept, the pressures of these great, mature motivations? It is the sense of common roots and common destiny with his or her parents. And these are profoundly cultivated in the framework of the Sabbath. The Jewish people is what it is because of patterns of thought and observance sustained over thousands of years. If these roots are allowed to disappear, so will their fruits; and the Jew and his gifts will be no more.

We are witnessing widening disorganization in family life. If marriages become increasingly insecure, with less and less enduring investment of mate in mate and parent in child, the general community may be able to muddle through and somehow survive. But the Jew will not. This little people, surrounded by a vast assimilating sea, endures only because it has special qualities. And these are nurtured and transmitted through a specially dedicated family life. Without it the game is up; the great dreams and splendorous contributions of this peculiar people will have come to an end.

In the social ecology of our day, the Jew is an endangered species. Jewish young people, who are properly agitated over the problems of ecology and the growing destruction of that natural world which enables life and beauty to continue, would do well to understand the threat to this rare genus, Jew, and use every resource at their command to keep him from becoming extinct.

If we shudder at that prospect, then we must determine to reverse the tide of the last generation, and commit ourselves to reinstitute the spirit and the forms of the Sabbath in our homes. Since this won't be spurred on by the kind of compulsion from the outside that Heinrich Heine depicts above, it must come from conviction on the inside. And since it won't just happen from ingrained habit as with our grandparents, it will have to be by new initiative and determination. We will feel self-conscious and strange at first. And we may find that we cannot change a whole pattern at once. But we must not be discouraged. The great Rabbi Leo Baeck, head of German Jewry, whose spirit helped thousands survive the terrors of the concentration camp, counseled us wisely: "Make a beginning, it can be small; only start, and let the Sabbath grow."

How profound are his words: "Make a beginning." There is no future for Judaism, nor for the Jew in the wider world, without the Sabbath in the home. Yet it is not to be expected that Jewry will speedily recapture the full, rich traditions of the whole Sabbath day. But we can all keep the seed of it alive and nurture it. And that is crucial. For once the seed is gone there is no hope. But with it there can be life anew.

To the blessings of the candles and the bread, still widely observed, we can add the simple blessing of the wine, then the whole Kiddush, and then learn to sing it. For nothing holds emotion and unites souls like song. We can augment this with the Zemirot, the informal melodies of the Sabbath table. We can sing increasing portions of the many-faceted blessing after the meal, the Bircat haMazon. And on Saturday, Havdala can seal the whole day. Only "make a beginning and let the Sabbath grow."

The Christian Home and the Christian Future

What of the future of the Christian faith? Its leaders are now saying that it, too, depends upon the recapturing of the home and the observances that join the generations. One acclaimed and challenging spokesperson is John H. Westerhoff III of Duke University Divinity School. In *Learning Through Liturgy*, he has written:

> The field work of anthropologist Gwen Neville in the area of informal or "folk liturgies" shows how the most formative and lasting religious education occurs not in the "heady" environment of the church school classrooms but in the highly charged liturgical context of daily, weekly and yearly events that celebrate themes that are at the heart of family religious belief structures.

Prof. Westerhoff pleads for ceremonies that unite the generations: "We cannot accept the separation of children and youth and adults. Community is the gift of shared rituals."

In study after study by Christian educators today, one finds this sense of urgency. Morton Kelsey opens his book *Can Christians Be Educated?* with the words: "The Christian Church has taken a terrific battering in recent years. There is a real question in many minds as to whether the tradition of faith can be passed on to modern men and women." High in priority among the solutions offered is the reaching of the child from the very beginning through the home and family life. "Early family life and background constitute the most powerful, persuasive and perduring variable affecting all phases of an individual's learning," we read in James Michael Lee's *The Flow of Religious Instruction.*

Following such critical insights, Catholic and Protestant communities have innovated wide programs of family education. Here sacred days and seasons of the religious year are celebrated with projects in the home. The whole family prays and studies and plays together. For "these are the opportunities when God's love is most dearly revealed in our family," declares the introduction to *The Family Book of Seasons.*

Jewish education has been similarly stimulated; witness the titles: *Parents Are Teachers, Too* and *Providing the Missing Link.* We are indeed learning from each other! Observe a charming symbol of this: the word "Shalom" (Hebrew for not just peace, but also wholeness, well-being) is often used in the titles and concepts of these liturgical ventures of the church, even as it has been the inseparable companion of "Shabbat" in Judaism.

VI

Sex and Maturity

SEX AND MATURITY

A man should spend less than his means
on food and drink for himself . . .
and above his means on honoring his wife and children.
—Talmud

Getting and Giving

LOVE-SEX ATTRACTION plays another role parallel to the religious experience. It is nature's way of summoning a man and woman up toward the full stature of their maturity. We are born self-centered. As infants we cry out for our needs, heedless of the convenience or burdens of others. We must, to survive. The process of outgrowing this essential immaturity is painful and very long. Step by step we learn that it is possible to be considerate of mother, to give up or delay some of our demands with the recognition that she has desires and needs of her own.

We discover that it is fun to help her, even as she

seems to get pleasure out of helping us. We learn how to play differently, not always insisting on winning and keeping for ourselves, but sometimes sharing and enjoying another's success. Thus we move, often through fits and starts, toward maturity, which is the ability to find our good in the good of another or of the group.

Then, when we fall in love, we are drawn to take a giant leap in this direction. We sing: "There's not a thing I wouldn't do for you"; and we feel it as a powerful instinctive reality. For if we are truly in love we find ourselves not only "caring" for another, but wanting to "take care" of the other, eager to do all in our power to advance his good, meet her need. What we must contribute to do this is perceived by us not as a sacrifice but as a joy. This is the hallmark of true maturation. Few reach this height perfectly; unredeemed islands of infantile self-centeredness remain. But unless one feels that his or her impulsion is predominantly to give to, rather than to get from, the other, one may be sure that it is really not love. This is the test, the answer to that question asked by young people.

The beauty is that love's propulsion toward maturity is cumulative. It can achieve its goal in a self-energizing upward spiral. We may begin with just the intimation of giving. But our love leads to revelation, and this in turn to a greater capacity for giving and receiving love. And all along, our mate, feeling more love, gives more.

The perfect symbol of this comes in the true sexual union. Here the giving of pleasure to another becomes the source of our reaching our own fullest joy. Indeed, the giving and the getting are inextricably interwoven.

The psychiatrist Rollo May writes in his volume,

Love and Will: "The paradox of love is that it is the highest degree of awareness of the self as a person at the same time that it is the highest degree of absorption in the other."

Eric Fromm meditates on the interrelation of psyche and soma:

Giving is the highest expression of potency. In the very act of giving, I experience my strength, my wealth, my power. This experience of heightened vitality fills me with joy. . . . The culmination of the male sexual function lies in the act of giving; the man gives himself, his sexual organ to the woman. At the moment of orgasm he gives his semen to her. He cannot help giving it if he is potent. If he cannot, he is impotent. . . . She gives herself too; she opens the gates to her feminine center; in the act of receiving, she gives. If she is incapable of this act of giving, if she can only receive, she is frigid. With her the act of giving occurs again, as a mother. She gives of herself to the growing child within her, she gives of her milk to the infant, she gives her bodily warmth. Not to give would be painful.

Creating New Worlds

God creates new worlds constantly. In what way?
By causing marriages to take place.
—Zohar

In a sense, marriage represents not only our maturation, but our elevation into a whole new world, unique for us in that it is of our own making. For the first time it is our decision, our taste and direction that

shape the environment in which we have our deepest
being. Rabbi Leo Baeck expressed it beautifully:

Union and the marriage which surrounds it, is like a second
creation. Man's first lot, his birth, has been drawn and prepared for him. He is born without his choice. But another
bond of equally fateful importance is effected by man himself,
his own will and doing. Together man and woman determine
for each other their whole lives' configuration, their place in
the world, their horizon. Two beings let their lives be born
into each other. Marriage becomes the second lot in life.

The Rabbis of old likewise looked upon this as a
second creation, meriting God's special concern scarcely
less than the first. The Midrash relates that a Roman
lady chided her friend, a Rabbi, that the God of Israel
is a lazy God: "What has He been doing since those
six days when he created the world?" "He has been
arranging marriages." "Is that an occupation! I could
do that myself." "You think it is simple? It is as difficult
for the Holy One as dividing the Red Sea." So she took
her thousand male slaves and thousand female slaves
and set them in rows and announced who would marry
whom. But the next day they came back with bruises
and broken bones, having rejected these mates. So she
summoned the Rabbi and confessed: "What you told
me is correct. There is no God like your God."

If it was hard then, what shall we say of our day,
with anthropologist Margaret Mead telling us that
American marriage "is one of the most difficult forms
the human race has ever attempted." But perhaps it
helps to know that it is worth it, since it is the creation
of our new world, our own self-determined life.

The Endless Cycle of Exciting Rewards

Superficial love can pall, become boring. "There's nothing new under the sun," wrote the world-weary Koheleth, author of Ecclesiastes (1:9). But deep love brings us into an endless cycle of ever-renewing, ever-exciting goals and pleasures.

The revelation of love itself is followed by the excitement of setting up a home which will foster the delight of our union. Then comes the awesome wonder of watching children being born and growing into Menschen—responsible, sensitive, whole human beings. We live a great portion of our days under the stimulating challenge—is there a profounder one on earth?—of drawing forth their talents and shaping their characters, healing their hurts, hoping with them their hopes. Throughout all these the delights of our physical-spiritual intimacy do not diminish but become only the more exquisitely meaningful. One parent told her counselor: "The pain and the happiness of these years of raising kids together has given us hundreds of experiences of sharing; we feel joined in so many areas that sex is often like a feast."

There is the fulfillment of observing the careers of one's offspring and their rewards, as well as the joy of their own marriages. Nachas Fun Kinder, we call it in Jewish life—the satisfaction from children. The profound humorist, Sam Levenson, said that early in his life he learned that Nachas Fun Kinder must be the chief purpose of living, since this is what his parents

and their friends wished one another more than any-
thing else.

From the children's mating comes a new thrill:
grandchildren. The perception that this is one of the
richest of all God's blessings is put into verse and song
by the Psalmist:

> May the Lord bless you from Zion
> And may you see the good of Jerusalem
>   all the days of your life.
> May you see your children's children,
> And peace upon Israel.
>   —Psalm 128:5–6

Here the seeing of one's children's children is given
a standing on a level with the longed-for satisfactions
of the welfare of the Holy City and peace for all Israel.

There is never a wearying; long before one pleasure
is ever taken for granted a new marvel looms on the
horizon, refreshing all the extant excitements as well.

The cycle goes on and on forever, as the children
look forward to their children's children. We are part
of the unending Grand Design. By participating in it
with enthusiasm and with the conscious awareness that
it is the Design, we affirm that life is good. This is the
gift of our love. Leo Baeck put it succinctly: "To be
born, to bear, and the tie of marriage which connects
the two . . . can be affirmed only together. They are
the great 'yea' of life, . . . the 'yea' which man replies
to his God."

Because we went out to greet life and to affirm it,
rather than waiting skeptically for it to come and prove
itself to us, we gained rewards on three concurrent

levels: our personal joys with our mate—which need never diminish—our joint delight in our children and theirs, and—as the Psalm above intimated—an abiding warmth in knowing that we are all part of the strength and hope of the eternal people of Israel, called to bless mankind.

The Seven Blessings of the wedding ceremony remind the Jewish couple from the very moment of their marriage that they are being united not for their private fulfillment alone, but for the grand continuum of Jewish life: "Blessed are You, O Lord, who cause Zion to rejoice in her children." Indeed, their marriage is taken as a symbol of Israel's joyful deliverance to come: "May there speedily be heard in the cities of Judah and in the environs of Jerusalem, the voice of joy and the voice of gladness, the voice of bridegrooms coming forth from their chambers." The phrases re-echo those of Jeremiah in his declaration of faith that though Jerusalem was about to be destroyed, it would ultimately be restored and there would again be heard the gladsome wedding sounds in Zion's courts (Jeremiah 33:10–11).

VII

Overcoming the Failure of Sex Today

Without God (Yod Heh),
  man (Aleph Yod Shin) and woman (Aleph Shin Heh)
  are reduced to a consuming fire (Aleph Shin).
                    —Talmud, Sota 17a

OVERCOMING THE FAILURE
OF SEX TODAY

Beyond the Sexual Revolution

WILL the world of love which we all try to build be rich in meaning and enthusiasm? Or will it betray our youthful dreams? The answer will be affected by our understanding of the sexual revolution which has swept over our age with unprecedented speed. It claims to have brought a new freedom, to have delivered us from outworn taboos. Sex, it affirms, is simply a natural, physical, private pleasure to be enjoyed, and not to be inhibited by negative attitudes toward "the flesh." This has an appeal to the spirit of freedom and self-determination of today's individuals.

Yet we find its followers turning away from it, complaining of loss of intimacy, romance, and meaning. This was the testimony of both popular surveys and professional counselors, even before the growing fear of sexually transmitted diseases.

Debora Phillips, Director of the Princeton Center for Behavior Therapy, has concluded: "Sex without commitment is losing its appeal. . . . College students, who generally forecast what will be happening in the general society, are seeking more value-laden relationships."

The error, they have discovered, is that sex simply is not simple. It cannot be separated from our whole complex being, with its interacting body and mind, emotions and ideals, tastes and even subtle visions of a better, surer self and a better world.

George Leonard, for many years senior editor of *Look* magazine, has told us how he first welcomed the sexual revolution and then saw how "in slaying some loathsome dragons, it has brought to light some formidable new ones." He concluded in his moving, love-exalting book, *The End of Sex*:

We need to discard the entire idea encoded in the present usage of the word "sex," along with the dangerous trivialization, fragmentation and depersonalization that it encourages. We need to reconnect the bedroom with the rest of our lives, to realize that the way we make love influences the way we make our world, and vice versa.

We need to reawaken to the almost endless, half-forgotten, life-transforming powers of full-bodied, fully committed erotic love.

Faith, Symbols, and Meaning

The children of Israel shall keep the Sabbath. . . .
It is a sign between Me
and the children of Israel forever.
—Exodus 31:16–17

A rare insight into the relation between faith and desire is revealed by Rollo May. Out of a lifetime of study and psychiatric counseling he writes that "emptiness" is the chief problem of people in our century. "Many therapists today rarely see patients who exhibit repression of sex. . . . What our patients do complain of is lack of feeling and passion. . . . So much sex and so little meaning or even fun in it."

Dr. May points to one of the causes of this "banalization of sex":

Lack of will, lack of zest in life, is due to lack of faith, which in part comes from severing one's self from the great symbolic experiences in the tradition of our historic culture. . . . Without faith we cannot want, we cannot wish; we become impotent, genitally as well as otherwise. Symbolism gives wish its specifically human quality; without this even the emotional and sexual aspects of wanting become dried up.

Sex is enhanced when life is affirmed and great purposes loom challengingly before us. We come to our mate to comfort and delight ourselves, it is true. But we come also to be partners in the mysterious experience of engendering new lives and of shaping them.

And through them we commit ourselves anew to the far-visioned tasks of our faith, whether it be "bringing the world to Christ," if we have been married in his name, or ensuring the faithfulness and survival of a people covenanted to be "a light unto the nations" (Isaiah 42:6), if we have been wed "according to the law of Moses and of Israel." The context of the Grand Design is life-giving, stimulating, fulfilling. Seeking more than pleasure, we are renewed, and the pleasure itself is deepened. Here the symbols of our historic cultures— whether we are moved by the Eucharist and the Cross, or by the Sabbath table and the Torah in the Ark—are powerful reminders of these higher purposes, never allowing us to forget the exalted realm in which we have our being.

Thought-Patterns of Permanence

The symbols we have described help us face the troubling threat of the impermanence of marriage today. Many a young person has resisted making this commitment because he has witnessed so much divorce. The anguish and depression that such tearing apart of our personal lives inflicts upon adults and children concerns our whole society.

There are influences all about us accustoming us to consider things temporary, replaceable. Change is rampant. Schools, career directions, jobs are readily abandoned for new ones. Millions move from their homes, uproot local ties every few years. Cars, possessions, conveniences are disposable. On every side, advertisements entice us to give up the old and use the "new, improved" product.

Loyalty seems to have lost its appeal. Even in sports, where cherished personalities were once the focus of hometown support, stars are so precipitously shifted and sold that the old teams are scarcely recognizable. Alvin Tofler, in his *Future Shock*, has described the bewildering array of these ever more whirling changes. Most seem bound to go on. Many indeed provide advantages. But the whole climate encourages the short-ranged, ego-centered view that plays havoc with stability in marriage: "I have to think of my own fulfillment. If I am not content now with my role, my mate, I'll find another. I have a right to be happy, now."

Even some young marriage counselors have fallen into this pattern. I have sent couples for expert guidance and been appalled to find a social worker laboring to get the husband to sort out his feelings as to whether or not he really wants the marriage, and the wife to prepare herself in case he leaves her. No attempt was made to have the couple consider the advantages to themselves and their children of a possible reconciliation. No time was set aside for a period in which to try to effect changes in conduct and attitude that might rekindle the true admiration and delight that had first brought them together.

We must somehow recapture thought-patterns of permanence, at least in the deepest aspects of our lives. How? By taking time from the kaleidoscopic practical world to contemplate the wondrous, even mysterious. The new may dazzle and amaze. But it is the ageless, the unchanging, that strikes us with awe. It is no accident that we call God "The Eternal One." And we bless Him "forever and ever." The Anglican prayer book translates this Hebrew more poignantly: "World without end."

One suffused with the awe of the enduring is himself more able to endure, more able to labor patiently for long-range, overarching fulfillments. One is fortified against the pitfall of "instant gratification."

True pleasure in the man-woman relationship is something that has to be cultivated, nutured with care and time, because it must grow, like a flower. It is not in the category of human creations which can be speeded up by our accelerating technology. It is rather a gift of nature, and her ever-gradual, eternal design. And as a *gift* it is *ours to receive*, and *not to take*. To try to reach out and seize the flower of love, to attempt to force it or hasten it, is to crush it.

> I adjure you, O daughters of Jerusalem,
> That ye awaken not, nor stir up love,
> Until it please.
>   —Song of Songs 3:5

Short-term love which seeks to escape obligation and involvement leads to shortchanged reward. "Free sex can hurt," writes Georgie Anne Geyer, and documents it in her widely read column. Long-visioned love welcomes the commitment and responsibility that so naturally come with it. It looks forward to the undiminishing delight when the pleasure principle is integrated with the Enduring Plan.

"Self-realization" can be a danger if it is pursued

without the understanding that the self is "realized" only in concerned relationship to others. This hallmark of maturity points the way to "meaning" in our existence. The uncommitted life becomes the empty life. Rabbi Samuel David Luzzatto, Italian bible scholar and philosopher of the last century, counseled in one of his wise letters: "The purpose of a young man is to take on obligations. For then he will have worries; and then he will be happy!"

The You That You Bring with You

> Can you believe that you and I
> are a state of mind?
> —Lois Wyse

An experience is not just an event that happens to you. It is also the you that you bring to the event. The apperceptive mass, the body of thoughts, the expectations and appreciations that we bring to it affect the very essence of what we see or feel. If we have no high points of reference, no great hopes, we are unlikely to have great experiences. A key function of religion is to raise our awareness and expectation. It seeks to exalt the way in which we look at each other. How different from "that's my sex-mate" is the thought: "that's my partner in searching out the meaning and savoring the rewards of this life." Charlotte and Howard Clinebell, marriage counselors, in their altogether inspiring volume, *The Intimate Marriage*, write: "No single factor does more to give a marriage joy than shared commitment to spiritual discovery."

Our chance of avoiding the emptiness of sex in our day is vastly increased if we have been spiritually sensitized from childhood on. If we have been encouraged to see beneath the obvious and the external, to sense the wonder of sea and stars, to listen to the speech of trees and stand in awe before an opening flower, then we are accustomed to seeking and finding insights all about. We are prepared to experience the full radiance of love.

We can sustain it more surely if we continue to keep our spiritual antennae alive to "the more" in nature, in poetry, in the arts, and in the widening reaches of human knowledge. The trick is to keep the film of "taking for granted" from settling on our perceptions. The Baal Shem Tov, founder of the joyous movement of Hasidism, insisted that we must learn to continue to see things "with eyes of the first time." Both science and faith provide wide areas in which we can practice this discipline. Loren Eiseley's *The Immense Journey*, which is anthropology lit with insight, is as effective here as any Psalm or prayer: "I can only report from my own wilderness. The important thing is that each man possess such a wilderness and that he consider what marvels are to be observed there." All worship is directed toward the encouragement of this mood. The new *Gates of Prayer* affirms: "We walk sightless among miracles. Lord, fill our eyes with seeing and our minds with knowing."

Transcending the Physical

The habit of seeking the "more" fortifies one against the trap of viewing sex primarily as a physical experience. The dangers here are many. Such a pattern can desensitize one and make one incapable of recognizing the subtler meanings of the man-woman potential.

The physical relationship itself may also be imperiled by this false emphasis. Harvey Gochros, in his volume, *Human Sexuality and Social Work*, has warned that a current cause of marital dysfunction is "the model of the sexual athlete." He deplores "preoccupation with the mechanical aspects of sexuality as depicted in many manuals" since it can lead to a focus on techniques rather than total satisfaction, to a loss of spontaneity and a pressure to "perform."

The contrast between superficial sex and true intimacy was expressed by the Rabbis in a striking fashion. They pointed out that in Hebrew man is *Ish* (spelled with the three letters: Aleph Yod Shin), and woman *Ishah* (Aleph Shin Heh). Take away God (Yod Heh), and all you have left in each of them is *Esh* (Aleph Shin) or a consuming fire.

But keep the sense of the Holy One, of transcendent meaning, and not only are the mystery and the glory there, but there is no need to "prove oneself" or to "keep score." For sex is then not a "game," pursued for itself; rather it is a communion. And the mere giving of a man and woman to each other touches a high realm of meaning and delight. Spiritually informed lovers afford each other such security that the ego of one is not crushed by a single sexual incompletion, or even several. And, far from placing blame, they encourage and console each other, thus taking away fear and pressure, which are primary causes of nonperformance.

Women's Liberation and the Interplay of the Arts

. . . listening together to the murmur of hidden meaning in music until the harmonies of what it means to be human pulse also in you.

—Ross Snyder

The admiration that one has for another as a unique individual with gifts that inspire adds wings to every phase of the relationship. From of old, the bible inculcated the habit of looking upon the woman not just as a wife, but as a complete person with special competences, dedication, and wisdom. Among the praises of the book of Proverbs we read:

She considers a field and buys it;
    With the fruit of her hands she plants a vineyard.
She perceives that her merchandise is good.
She lays her hands to the distaff,
    All her household are clothed with scarlet.
She extends her hands to the poor.
Strength and dignity are her clothing,
    And she laughs at the time to come.

She opens her mouth with wisdom,
And the law of kindness is on her tongue.

Note that the tributes here are not only to the economic and artistic talents, but to the spiritual contributions of the woman. The Rabbis affirmed time and again that hers is a key role in keeping faith alive in the homes and in the people of Israel. The twenty-fourth chapter of Genesis tells us that after Sarah died, Isaac took Rebecca into the home as his bride. "And Isaac was comforted for his mother" (24:67). One commentator explained that on each Sabbath, Sarah, the first mother in Israel, had been able to make the spirit of God luminous in the dwelling. When she departed, so did that aura. But when Rebecca came, she restored it.

In one of the stories of the Rabbis we read that a pious man was married to a pious woman. But since they had no children they divorced, in order to fulfill the commandment to multiply (Genesis 1:28). He went forth and married a wicked woman, and she made him wicked. She went forth and married a wicked man, but she made him righteous. "It follows that all depends upon the woman," declared the sages.

Rabbi Jose said touchingly: "Never have I called her my wife, but always 'my home.' "

The Talmud delights in telling how Beruriah, the wife of Rabbi Meir, demonstrated such wisdom and such skill in rabbinic interpretation that she was able to persuade and correct her learned husband. Once he was so troubled by the evil men in his neighborhood that he prayed that they should die. But she turned to him and asked: "What are you thinking of? Is it that it is written: 'Let sinners cease out of the earth' [Psalm 104:35]? But the text can also be read to mean: 'Let sins cease out of the earth.' Therefore pray that these men repent and be no longer wicked. For that is the true meaning of the end of the verse: 'Let the wicked be no more.' " So Rabbi Meir prayed on their behalf and they repented.

This is not meant to imply that Judaism always afforded an equal role and status to the feminine sex. It did not. But what is remarkable is that even in an ancient era of male domination in all fields, its teachings served to enhance the dignity and appreciation accorded womanhood.

The long-grounded Jewish pattern of respecting women and rejoicing in their talents can be a valuable asset today. For the liberation of women, who are now reaching out for creativity and careers in the panoply of human endeavors, has been viewed by some men as a disturbing factor in their marriage, unsettling their accustomed office of provider, and of representative to the larger world. Some consider that their male role has been demeaned, and that this dims their marriage, and casts a pall over their sexual fulfillment as well.

There can be no doubt that having two careers in a family will entail adjustments, requiring flexibility with perhaps some sharing of roles. But these need not be viewed as a threat to the delight of the relationship. On the contrary, the more talented and achieving a woman is, the more exciting and desirable she can be in the total life picture, including her oneness with her mate, even as his talents are part of the reward that he brings to her. For their intimacy partakes of added artistry, and of appreciation for the unique, developing facets now offered in love by each to the other. Even the simple sharing of home duties may add to the tenderness.

Lovemaking, in the Hebrew idiom, as we learned early in the book, means to "know" another. "And Adam knew his wife." How fascinating when that other has many qualities to know. How instructive: that each one should make sure that he or she keeps growing, keeps perfecting attributes and commitments that make one ever more desirable to know.

We may take our cue from an unusual concept which Marcel Proust and the continental exponents of art relished at the turn of the century. They called it synesthesia, signifying the effect of one sense calling forth associations in another. Thus a painting might summon forth a certain melody, or a color evoke a particular poem.

There is indeed an interplay of the arts. And nowhere is it more ready and rewarding than in the interplay of the art of loving and all the other quests for beauty and excellence. The enjoyment which a couple finds together in music almost inevitably adds notes of grace to their pleasure in each other's arms. Often a particular melody becomes their special call to love. And caresses may be considered a pizzicato.

Shared achievements, or the creation by one with appreciation by the other, in painting, dancing, performing, or even praying, are profound stimulants to erotic expression and reward. Some may recall the famous advertisement of a perfume which depicted the violinist interrupting his musical ecstacy by sweeping his pianist up into his arms.

The emancipation of woman opens the way for the maturing of love, grounded on the equal respect of the sexes and the merging of total personalities abounding in physical, spiritual, and intellectual gifts. And the biblical-rabbinic tradition that makes man and woman utter partners in their search for God, and in the revelation that comes to them when they are one, can help guide the way to that fulfillment.

VIII

The Mystic Doctrine
of Oneness

Israel, the Holy One, blessed be He,
and the Torah are one.
— Zohar, Ahare 73a

THE MYSTIC DOCTRINE
OF ONENESS

The Hunger for Unity

WE HAVE sometimes referred to the "mystery" of marriage, and often to "mystics." Who are they? In general a mystic is one who believes in the possibility of attaining knowledge through insight that is beyond ordinary seeing and reasoning. Indeed, what we have been writing all along has an element of mysticism in it, in that it draws you to experience that which is Beyond. It is fascinating to observe that whether this mysticism is found in some secular poets and philosophers, as indeed it is, or in religious literature, where we expect it, the goal is strikingly the same: to attain a sense of overarching *unity*.

Consider again the words of Alan Watts, identifying the unique joy of the union of man and woman with "the delight which inheres in life itself, in our funda-

mental but normally unrealized identity with the world."
Or the further expressions of George Leonard:

Love is a human expression of the creative force that grows great forests, that calls primeval creatures from the sea, to breathe, to run, to fly. It is the force that gives life to human individuals and then joins them together into families and tribes and nations and that must eventually unify all the world.

The central theme of the mystical movement which once emerged in Judaism is likewise "oneness," or Yihud in Hebrew. The teachings were known as Kabbala, that is "the receiving" (of the tradition). Judaism discouraged speculation on how God and His world "operate in their inner nature, knowable to but a few," insisting as the Torah says that the earth is given to man, but "the secret things belong to the Lord" (Deuteronomy 29:28).

Yet mystic groups arose in every age. The greatest of these were the Kabbalists. Their chief book, Zohar (meaning splendor), "succeeded in establishing itself for three centuries, from about 1500 to 1800 [C.E.], as a source of doctrine and revelation equal in authority to the Bible and the Talmud."

Although many of its details may appear strange to us today, the directions in which it points and searches can strike a note of kinship within us and add to our wisdom. Rabbi Abraham Joshua Heschel described its spirit perceptively:

To the analytical mind, the universe is broken apart. It is split into the known and the unknown, into the seen and the unseen. But, in the mystic contemplation all things are seen as one. . . . The Kabbalists knew that what their senses perceive is but the jutting edge of what is deeply hidden. Extending over into the invisible, the things of this world stand in a secret contact with that which no eye has ever perceived. . . . All things below are symbols of that which is above. . . . You grasp the essence of the here by conceiving the beyond.

All of Judaism, as we know, stresses the principle of Unity. The watchword of the faith is the Shema, which pronounces God One. But the Zohar goes further and declares that the Jew not only proclaims Him One, but helps to make Him and His world One. Thus the Kabbalists liked to call the Jewish people "HaMe-Yahadim," which is not an adjective but an active verb, meaning "those who make [God and His world] One."

How does the Jew do this? By observing the Mitzvot, the commandments of God, with a high and holy intention, conscious of their cosmic import. For they have impact not only upon humanity here on earth, but especially upon the Divine Economy in heaven. Since the universe is woven of one fabric, what happens below influences critically what happens above, facilitating or obstructing the purposes, indeed the very reign, of the Almighty.

This principle the Kabbalists applied to all the injunctions of the Torah, ever stressing that it is not just the outward deed but the accompanying purity and direction of thought that achieve the grand result.

The holiness of intention in the relation between man and woman was considered of special import. It is understandable that the mystics of many faiths, in seeking to fathom and conceive the hidden principles by which this fantastic world of ours functions, should have turned to the sexual experience with its transporting ecstacy, its manifold overtones for the individual, and its cosmic import as an instrument in the continuity of life itself. The idea developed that the male-female design permeates the whole creation and provides a clue to its workings.

The Zohar here asserted that man is not "one," he is not complete and whole, unless he is united with woman. The classic rabbinic legend affirms that the souls in heaven, waiting to be born, are stored not singly but in pairs, in spheres composed of a male and a female. Before birth these are separated and the male soul put into the body of a boy and the female into that of a girl, who as they mature spend years searching until they find their predesigned other half with whom they can be complete again. The Zohar declared that without that union man is not even called man, nor does God's presence rest upon him to bless him. It refers to the verse: "Male and female He created them, and blessed them, and called their name Adam [man]" (Genesis 5:2). Since it says *their* name and not *his* name, it signifies that man is not man except in that union. "The Shechina (Divine Presence) can rest only on a married man, because an unmarried man is but half a man, and the Shechina does not rest upon that which is imperfect."

But when this union is achieved in truth and in consecration to its exalted purpose, not only does it make man and woman complete, it helps to make the whole Order, seen and unseen, complete.

The mystics of the Zohar related this to an ancient

perplexity with which they were concerned: How can God, who is all spirit, have contact with and rule over the world, which is essentially physical? The Greek philosophers speculated that there are ten emanations, or spheres, issuing down from God, each becoming progressively less spiritual and more physical, until the last is able to make contact with this lowly earth. One might think of a great electric generator, whose gigantic power has to be stepped down through a series of transformers before it can be put into ordinary usage.

The Kabbalists pictured these spheres as really being ten aspects of the Holy One, considered as it were as separate entities; and they gave to each a Hebrew name, depicting a characteristic of the Almighty. Since the male-female principle pervades all, they attributed to some a masculine nature and to some a feminine. One of the latter is the Shechina, the Indwelling or Presence of God. And they speculated that when these spheres are joined, the Divine Order is in harmony, and the stream of God's blessings can flow unimpeded into His universe, giving direction and fulfillment.

In the interaction of the upper and the lower realms, the union in utter love and holy intention of man and woman on earth can facilitate the joining of the celestial principles on high and thus help God to rule his world. "In the Kabbala," wrote Gershon Scholem, "every true marriage is a symbolic realization of the union of God and the Shechina."

The Kabbalists were aware that this deep speculation might seem strange to the ordinary person. Although sympathetic to Kabbala, Nachmanides, in depicting it for a friend, himself called it "esoteric" and warned him: "Guard this mystery without revealing it to any man."

Today we do not think in terms of these ancient metaphysical problems and their speculative solutions. Yet there is much that we can learn from these mystics. We must be impressed by the crucial role which they assigned to the man-woman relationship in the whole scheme of things, and their insistence that only through its sanctity can the world function properly. Let us put it into the sociological terms of our day: Only when husband and wife combine physical and spiritual harmony can they provide the family security needed to raise their child to the full ethical potential that God seeks of him. And as the child is led forth, so the world is built. In this sense, indeed, only when there is high-intentioned union of man and woman can God and His world become one.

But let us keep a portion of the mystic element as well: In these days of marital restlessness and divorce, what can sustain the stability we long for? Is it not the sense that our oneness as man and woman is a deep part of the whole Grand Design, an experience beyond words or refutation that gives intimation of the Oneness that is secure, eternal!

The Kabbalists gave the name of "Raza de Shabta"—the Hidden Secret of the Sabbath—to the culmination of their speculations, namely that the Sabbath is the most appropriate time for man and woman to be united, not only for their sake, but for the sake of the influence they exert on the Divine Economy itself, for this is the day of the union of the King with the Shechina. This was their way of conceiving the interrelation of sex, God, and the Sabbath.

How to Make Love

Out of such thinking came not just theories, but practical counsel of great wisdom and tenderness. We quote the following from Nachmanides' "Epistle on Holiness," which sought to guide his friend on how to approach the "holy act," namely sex:

(Although written from the male viewpoint—all books were written by men in those days—it can provide similar grace in the initiative and active role taken by the woman. For Jewish tradition affirms also her joy and need in sex. Thus the bible declares that: "When a man has taken a bride he shall not go out with the army nor be assigned to it for any purpose; he shall be exempt one year for the sake of his household, to give happiness to the woman he has married" (Deuteronomy 24:5). And both bible and Mishna protect the "conjugal rights" of the wife.)

During the time of your intimate union with your wife do not act frivolously, in a trivializing and mocking manner, nor treat your wife derisively. But relate to her with dignity and respect.

Therefore first introduce her into the mood with gentle words that excite her emotion, appease her mind and delight her with joy. Thus you unite your mind and intention with hers. Say to her words which in part arouse in her passion, closeness, love, will, and erotic desire, and in part evoke in her reverence for God, piety and modesty. . . .

Never impose yourself upon her nor force her. For any sexual union without an abundance of passion, love and will, is without the Divine Presence. Do not quarrel with her nor act violently whenever coitus is involved. The Talmud says 'A lion ravishes and then eats and has no shame. So acts the brute: He hits and then cohabits and has no shame.' Rather court and attract her to you first with gracious and seductive, as well as refined and gentle words, so that both your intentions be for the sake of God. . . .

Do not hurry in arousing passion. Prolong till she is ready and in a passionate mood. Approach her lovingly and passionately, so that she reaches her orgasm first.

The Zohar recommended that upon preparing for the marital union one should offer a prayer affirming that "I garb myself in the holiness of the Divine King." And to this Nachmanides added such sentiments as "O Lord, let there be no weakness, unseemly thought or confusion of mind to prevent me from fulfilling my desire with my wife."

The Oneness in Terms of Today

The great, overall doctrine of Unity developed by the mystics of Judaism should have instructive appeal to men and women today as it did before. Even those whose rationalistic inclination turns them away from the metaphysical can join in affirming and serving their fundamental principle.

Everything in this world hungers for unity. The seed

longs and reaches for the sun, the bee for the flower, the soil for the rain, the river for the sea, God for His creatures, and His creatures for God. Perhaps the love relationship is so ecstatic because it is the human epitome and paradigm of the yearning for oneness that pervades the entire cosmos.

Can we not say that the essential pain in this world is the anguish of separation? Are not the ills before us occasioned by the separation of man from man, race from race, nation from nation? Of humankind from soil and nature? Of work from a sense of creativity and completion? Of sex from love, and love from commitment, and marriage from children, and all these from God?

"The basis for our need to love," writes Eric Fromm, "lies in the experience of separateness and the resulting need to overcome the anxiety of separateness by the experience of union."

Can we not agree that what is needed, as the Kabbalists insisted, is that Unity (Yihud) must be understood not as a passive state, but as an active, aggressive principle, by which we can affect and heal the world through practicing it in thought and deed!

An exalted partnership of husband and wife can teach us the fruits of such an affirmation. By understanding the implications of their action, a man and a woman, joined as one, striving to attain a perfect spiritual and physical union, can, through sex, not only become one with each other, but one with God. And by earnestly cherishing the Sabbath, which celebrates the meaning of that love, they can strengthen that oneness, not only with each other, but with their children, and with their people, and with its role as teacher of mankind, hastening the day when "the Lord shall be One, and His name shall be One," for all humanity shall be made One.

Sex—God—Sabbath held as One reveal the mystery of Jewish marriage. Indeed, they are close to revealing the heart and mystery of all of Judaism.

Seeking the Wider Oneness

We are coming toward the end of this "celebration." Indeed, we have here a package, often of things which at first may seem diverse, from the Sabbath of the ancient Hebrews to the marriage encounter created by the modern Church; from the depth-seeking testimonies of psychiatrists to the high-flying mystics of the Kabbala. But there is a thread that is woven throughout. That is the surge toward the wider oneness emerging in the searching hearts of today.

Once philosophers made grave distinctions between sacred and profane love, between spiritual love and the physical love that was said to detract from it. So the intimate affection of man and woman was looked upon somehow as separate from our religious life, and thus weakened. Now we see that it is not so, for the two loves are continuous. Truly understood, human love with its ecstacy is a revelation of the love of God, an overawing, irrefutable evidence of His Grand Design, a fundamental of His creation, leading to life. It is the great, natural stepping-stone to unshakable faith. And faith, in turn, with its exalted thoughts and beautiful, recurrent observances, is the natural servant of love. It brings into our days the celebrations that never let us forget to tend this precious sacred fire.

Once we wondered: should science or religion heal our souls? Now in the marriage encounter one can scarcely see where psychology ends and faith begins. Once it was asked: which religion will triumph to bring salvation to mankind? In the revitalized celebrations of marriage today we observe leaders of the many faiths sustaining one another, great traditions learning one from another.

Through all the perplexities of our time, the mystic union of man and woman, inspiring assurance and the upbeat vision of the home, stands as a symbol that there can yet be a life that glows with reward and celebration for the individual, and a good world, one world, God's world, for mankind.

EPILOGUE

A Personal Validation

He who finds a good wife
finds the essence of goodness.
—Proverbs 18:22

A PERSONAL VALIDATION

AS I THINK BACK over my forty-three years of
wedded life with my beloved Frances, who has
passed away, and for whom this book is a record
and tribute, I observe that the Sabbath has been our
theme song, woven in and out, capturing the deepest
moments and the highest reaches of our lives.

I was raised in a Reform Jewish home in Cleveland,
at a time when home observances were minimal. But
my mother had an unwavering and luminous sense of
God, which apparently she transmitted to me.
Throughout her eighty-seven years, she kept ten minutes of prayer—from Reform's Union Prayer Book—
inviolate and uninterruptible each morning. Temple at-
tendance was also an unbroken habit, regardless of
weather. She abstained from any kind of work, sewing,
or shopping on the Sabbath. At home she lit the candles
at the Friday evening table, and we blessed the bread.

At the Hebrew Union College I sensed that these
two ceremonies were not enough, so I learned to chant

the Kiddush. My marriage to Frances, four days before my ordination, was the occasion for members of the family to give us beautiful symbols for the Sabbath table. Fortified with these, on the first Sabbath in our own apartment, Frances and I conducted the blessings. From that moment on, the Sabbath prayers became the sign and symbol of our love. Indeed, a picture which I took of her blessing the candles, radiant and exalted, has always been the vision that I hold most tenderly of her beauty and essence.

But there was something else. From that first occasion on, the prayers became a wonderful avenue of communication by which soul opened to soul. For over the treetops of the traditional expressions, we found ourselves transmitting to each other, without saying a word, the feelings we shared most deeply at that moment, that week, that stage in our lives: Our soaring joy in each other. Our prayers: That we might have children. That the coming Holy Days might go well. That the sickness of a dear one might be healed. That the hurt that we gave to the other might be understood and forgiven and never repeated. That our love might flourish above all. The formal prayers were like a carrier wave in radio, which opens a path in the ether along which the modulations of the individual messages are brought through.

The coming of our first son, Jonathan, added to the glow of celebration about the table. And it wasn't long before the Sabbath observance proved its power even in a little child. Now it happened that our young friend, Hulda, who helped us with the baby on weekday afternoons, had somehow failed to go to church that morning, though it was a Holiday of Obligation in the Catholic Calendar. Her conscience overpowered her as she took Jon, then three, on his walk, and she kept going until she reached her sanctuary for worship. Upon her return, she told us what she had done and pleaded: "I hope you didn't mind." It was too late to mind. But we did inquire: "How did he act?" "Oh, he was wonderful. I unzipped his snowsuit and he stood beside me, perfectly quiet. Except that once in a while he looked up at the candles and said: 'Shabbas! Hulda, Shabbas!' "

With David, our second son, the experience was different, but no less instructive. Some little mazzik or demon in his head impelled him, over a prolonged, obnoxious period of his growing up, to sabotage the Sabbath observance. Never too content to remain immobile, he would rock the chair during the ceremony, or accidently jar the table and spill the wine. This was scarcely conducive to holy feelings. But we persevered. We made Shabbas, whatever David did or didn't do at the table.

Now David went off to college. On his first trip home what he wanted most was to chant the Kiddush! And he did it with boundless gusto! The mazzik within had become tired and departed. We had won out because we had stuck to our guns. What a lesson for parents!

The Kiddush now became a cherished symbol for David, too. He moved us to tears at the Bris (circumcision) of his first child, Jason. After the formal ceremony, he gathered us about the table with the wine cups and sang the whole Kiddush. Then he said: "My

father, in his book, *Return to Prayer*, advises that on
Shabbat the husband should bless and praise the wife.
This is like a Sabbath of joy for us, and I'd like to do
just that from this little volume." Putting his arm around
the new mother, he began:

> Eshet Chayil Mi Yimtza?
> A Woman of valor, who can find? . . .
> —Proverbs 31:10

His eyes welled up, his voice broke. "I don't know if
I can do this," he said. We wept, too, unashamed. But
he gulped and continued:

> The heart of her husband trusts in her
> And he has no lack of reward, . . .
> Grace is deceitful and beauty is vain,
> But a woman that reveres the Lord,
>   she shall be praised.
> —Proverbs 31:11, 30

It was the most touching use of the book that I could
have imagined.

A year and a half later, we put his charming picture
of Jason holding his little Kiddush Cup, on the lap of
his daddy with the father Kiddush Cup, up on the wall
of the dinette. From there it has smiled on our Sabbath
table and made more vivid the words which Frances
had for years appended to the candle blessings: "May
these lights bring health and happiness into our home
and the homes of our children during the coming week."

In a deep sense we lived from Shabbat to Shabbat,
where the moments of meaning were distilled and the
drafts of God's joys deeply savored. It was around the

Sabbath table that our daughters-in-law-to-be were first welcomed into the bosom of the family. It was here that we celebrated when our children and the members of the wider family came to town. And when the scourge of cancer cast its shadow over my dear one, it was here, too, that we poured out to each other, in the magical, shortwave silence that hovers over the text, all the depth of our prayers for healing and for courage.

Sabbath—again the Sabbath—was the focus which summoned forth the last strength and creative energies of Frances, as she prepared a picture–story book of "Thirty Years of a Rabbi and His Pulpit," to form the basis for the Sabbath programs that would celebrate my elevation to Founding Rabbi of Temple Emanu El.

At that time she was thrilled to have the whole family from their various cities meet together with all the little ones for the first time. Where? At the Sabbath table in our home. That afternoon my sons had read to her the words they had written to present on the weekend, words of homage and gratefulness to their father, and to their mother especially, for inspiring their values and the constant quest for beauty in their lives. And Raphy and Benjy, my older grandchildren, gave her a preview of the charming song that they arranged to perform together. All these built up the wonderful sense of fulfillment which she radiated as she blessed the candles at that unforgettable Sabbath table. None of us had ever said or felt the Shehechyanu—blessing God for having kept us alive and brought us to that day—more profoundly.

Again it was the Sabbath—that particular Sabbath—that prompted her to write, two weeks later, after an interval of pain, a remarkable letter to the Sisterhood. These last words of her life, penned on the very eve of her final trip to the hospital, were a veritable Legacy of Faith, like the *Ethical Wills* of the Rabbis:

Dear Friends of the Sisterhood Board:

How can I describe what a wonderful weekend of love and devotion all of you made possible for Rabbi Green and me. I knew that I would not be able to participate outside of the home. I had prayed for only one thing, that I would be able to be part of the beautiful Shabbat dinner we had before the services.

The good Lord was so good to me. I was able to get dressed and sit at the table with all of my dear ones. Your delicious basket of fruit had arrived earlier and we enjoyed it for dessert.

This has been a very trying time for all of my family. . . . I would like to take this opportunity to try to help some of you face up to terminal illness.

There are really two different people involved. One is Frances Green with a sick body. There is nothing I can do about that but have faith in my doctors and the new medical miracles. But the real Frances Green is the person I have always been—with plans, drives, projects, so much to do and plan. This is the Frances Green that needs your prayers and concern. Nothing is so important as the hope one gains from the knowledge that her friends are pulling and praying for her. A little note, a call . . .

I do so believe in the power of prayer. It revitalizes one. . . . Never hesitate, wondering, "What shall I say, what can I say?" Just say what's in your heart.

You know, dear friends, dying is a part of living. And I've been such a lucky, blessed person . . . had such a wonderful life: a devoted husband of almost 43 years; two beautiful, successful sons with their lovely wives; three grandchildren, talented, loving and the source of so much joy; and the feeling that in my own way I have made some contribution to my community, my temple and my family. I have no regrets, just thankfulness for all my blessings.

And lots of hope. Who knows, I may yet lick this crazy disease and have some very happy times with my "founding rabbi" and all of you.

God bless you,
Frances

The letter was read to the Sisterhood Board the next week when it was known that she was already losing ground in the hospital. You can imagine its impact!

My sons had come to town to relieve me, for I had been taken home exhausted. They told me that their families were coming in on Friday. I wondered and worried: how would I get any rest with all the children about? But they were quiet; even the little ones took care of one another. The news came that Frances had breathed her last, hard-fought, oxygen-deficient breath. She was at peace. Later in the afternoon, I got up. I was hungry and sat down in the dinette to munch some bread and butter. All at once I realized that Louise and Linda, my daughters-in-law, were bringing in the candles from the other room; my sons brought in the twisted Challa and the wine; and the children, the Kiddush cups. They kindled the lights, said the blessing, and sang. I had not asked them to. No, they had come in from their faraway homes, specifically to make Shabbas for me! For us! To bring its comfort and its strength.

At the funeral service on Sunday, Rabbi Hachen had beautifully pictured us about that Sabbath table, saying in our hearts: "Frances, we miss you." Not quite so. No one felt that Frances was missing. She was there. Absolutely there! We were blessing her candles, singing her song, adding her special phrase, chanting the Kiddush, which she shared, and she was singing right along with us. Nothing else could have kept her presence so surely among us. The mystery of Shabbat had transcended death and vanquished grief!

Each week it continues to do so. Even with the family away, Shabbat means to me the singing of her songs, her blessings, her sense of being blessed. Her presence, her gifts are there before me. And I am comforted, for I know that I too have been blessed. Such is the power of Shabbat for a Jewish man and woman who have shared love!

FOR FURTHER READING

You can pursue more deeply the concepts of this volume and find help in carrying out its suggested observances by browsing through the wide literature available. Here are notes on particular selections:

The Sabbath, by Abraham Joshua Heschel, Farrar, Straus & Giroux, New York, 1975. Depicts the full richness of Shabbat, and the symbolism of human love in Judaism.

This Is My God, by Herman Wouk, Doubleday, New York, 1959. The celebrated author writes movingly of the impact of Jewish tradition upon his personal life.

Love and Sex: A Modern Jewish Perspective, by Robert Gordis, Farrar, Straus & Giroux, New York, 1978. A comprehensive analysis of our theme by the eminent scholar and spokesman of Conservative Judaism.

Everyman's Talmud, by Abraham Cohen, Schocken Books, New York, 1975. Abundant, well-arranged, and delightfully readable selections of stories and teachings from the rabbinic literature.

Tadrich, The Sabbath Manual, Central Conference of American Rabbis, New York, 1972. Ceremonies and songs introduced by a wrestling with Sabbath values and decisions from a Reform point of view. (Out of print.)

Return to Prayer, by Alan S. Green, Union of American Hebrew Congregations, New York, 1971. "A Starter Set on the Road Back," with interpretation, transliteration, and Hebrew charts joined to observances and melodies. (Out of print.)

The Jewish Catalog, by Michael Strassfeld et al., Jewish Publications
Society of America, Philadelphia, 1973. Adds creative, do-it-
yourself artistry to observance. Pages 103–15 are on the Sabbath.

The Jewish Way in Love and Marriage, by Maurice Lamm, Harper &
Row, 1982. A wide-ranging, readable account of the rich back-
ground of this subject, relating it as well to current problems.
See especially Chapter 3 on "The Sexual Component," and
Chapters 7, 8, and 9 with wisdom applied to today.

In addition there are books referred to in the text
which one would do well to examine more completely,
such as:

The Marriage Encounter—As I Have Loved You, by Fr. Chuck Gallagher,
S.J., Doubleday and Co., Inc., Garden City, New York, 1975.
Written with great fervor, it blends religious insights and psy-
chological skills. Those who seek to know more about the techniques of the movement, its history, growth, and adoption by
different religious groups can turn to *Marriage Encounter,* by Don
Demarest, Jerry and Marilyn Sexton, Carillon Books, St. Paul,
1977. See especially Chapter 8, "The Ecumenical Thrust." (Both
books out of print.)

Learning Through Liturgy, by Gwen K. Neville and John H. Westerhoff III, Winston Press, Minneapolis, 1983; as well as *Generation
to Generation, Conversations on Religious Education and Culture,* by
Westerhoff and Neville, Pilgrim Press (The United Church Press),
New York, 1979.

The End of Sex—Erotic Love after the Sexual Revolution, by George
Leonard, Houghton, Mifflin, Co., Boston, 1983. A searching of
profound thoughts, touched with a sense of life's mystery and
wholeness, and of personal experience by a persuasive, literate
author. (Out of print.)

NOTES AND REFERENCES

INTRODUCTION

PAGE xii. "With every breath . . ." This is the author's interpretive translation of the original Hebrew.

I. Sex as Design

PAGE 6. *Iggeret HaKodesh, The Holy Letter*, translated by Seymour J. Cohen, Ktav Publishing House, New York, 1976, p. 40. Here I have used a different translation of the title, namely, *Epistle on Holiness*, since it is more clearly expressive of the author's title and intention. This is the title employed by Zvi A. Yehuda in his translation of selections from *Iggeret HaKodesh* (to be published). I appreciate Professor Yehuda's kind permission to use and quote from his manuscript.

PAGE 7. William H. Masters and Virginia E. Johnson, *The Pleasure Bond*, Little, Brown and Co., Boston, 1974.

PAGE 10. Alan Watts, *Nature, Man, and Woman*, Pantheon Books, a Division of Random House, New York, 1958, pp. 188–89 (see also pp. 203–4).

II. Sex as Revelation

PAGE 15. "A very flame of the Lord." This is a literal translation that has been used for many centuries by the English-speaking peoples, and has had its impact in this form. In the Hebrew idiom it signifies more simply a majestic flame.

PAGE 16. "For without it . . ." Midrash, Genesis Rabba 9:7.

PAGE 16. "The unmarried live . . ." Talmud, Yevamot 62b. (The reference is always to the Bavli, or Babylonian Talmud, unless otherwise noted.)

PAGE 16. "No man without woman . . ." Midrash, Genesis Rabba 22:2.

This has sometimes been used as an appropriate inscription on the Ketuva (marriage document).

III. *Pleasure as a Gift of God*

PAGE 23. "Man will have to . . ." Talmud Yerushalmi (Jerusalem Talmud), Kiddushin 4:9,66d.

PAGE 26. David R. Mace, *Hebrew Marriage, A Sociological Study*, Epworth Press, London, 1953. p. 263. Reprinted by permission of David R. Mace.

PAGE 27. "No one should think . . ." *Iggeret HaKodesh, The Holy Letter*, translated by Seymour J. Cohen, pp. 40, 42, 48. Also Maimonides, *Moreh Nevuchim, Guide to the Perplexed*, vol. II:36.

PAGE 28. Song of Songs: 1:1–2,13; 5:1; 6:3; 5:10–11, 14–15; 7:2–4; 8:6.

IV. *Reliving the Honeymoon Every Week*

PAGE 33. Al Nakawa, *Menorat HaMaor*, 2, p. 119.

PAGE 36. *Shaare Tefilla, Gates of Prayer*, The New Union Prayer Book, Central Conference of American Rabbis, New York, 1956, p. 205.

PAGE 38. Masters and Johnson, *The Pleasure Bond*, pp. 74–75.

PAGE 41. Father Chuck Gallagher, S. J., *The Marriage Encounter*, Doubleday and Co., Garden City, New York, 1975, pp. 14, 38.

V. *Recovering the Home as a Fountain of Faith*

PAGE 43. Ahad Ha-am, *Al Parashat Derachim*, HaShiloach 1898, III, p. 79; or Devir edition, Tel Aviv 1949, Bk. III, p. 286.

PAGE 47. Esther Oshiver Fisher, *Help for Today's Troubled Marriages*, Hawthorn Books, New York, 1968, p. 136.

PAGE 47. Heinrich Heine, quoted in *The Jewish Family*, edited by Benjamin Schlesinger, University of Toronto Press, 1971, p. 9.

PAGE 48. Joseph M. Yoffey, Introduction to *Jewish Marriage*, edited by Peter Elman, Soncino Press, London, 1967, p. 5.

PAGE 51. "The field work of Anthropologist . . ." John H. Westerhoff III, *Learning Through Liturgy*, The Seabury Press, New York, 1978, p. 102. Reprinted by permission of Harper & Row, Publishers Inc.

PAGE 51. "We cannot accept . . ." ibid., p. 103.

PAGE 51. "The Christian Church . . ." Morton Kelsey, *Can Christians Be Educated?* Religious Education Press, Mishawaka, Indiana, 1977, p. 5. Note another book and its striking title: *The Case Against Formal Religious Education:*

Children, Church and God, by Robert O'Neil and Michael Donovon, Corpus Books, New York and Cleveland, 1970.

PAGE 51. "Early family life . . ." James Michael Lee, *The Flow of Religious Instruction,* Religious Education Press, Mishakawa, Indiana, 1973, p. 60. Note how John H. Westerhoff continually elaborates this theme; see his *Generation to Generation, Conversations on Religious Education and Culture,* Pilgrim Press, 1974, p. 45 and elsewhere.

PAGE 52. *The Family Book of Seasons,* Our Sunday Visitor, Noll Plaza, Huntington, Indiana, 1981.

PAGE 52. Deborah Reshotko, *Parents Are Teachers, Too,* Union of American Hebrew Congregations, New York, 1985.

PAGE 52. *Providing the Missing Link,* Melton Research Center, the Jewish Theological Seminary of America, New York, 1986.

VI. *Sex and Maturity*

PAGE 55. "A man should spend . . ." Talmud, Hulin 84b.

PAGE 56. Rollo May, *Love and Will,* W.W. Norton and Company, New York, 1969, p. 311.

PAGE 57. Eric Fromm, *The Art of Loving,* Harper & Row, New York, 1956, pp. 23–24.

PAGE 57. "God creates new worlds . . ." Zohar I, p. 89a.

PAGE 58. Leo Baeck, quoted in *Marriage and the Jewish Tradition,* by Stanley Brav, Theosophical Library, New York, 1951, p. 122.

PAGE 58. "The Midrash relates . . ." Genesis Rabba 68:4.

PAGE 58. Margaret Mead, *Male and Female,* William Morrow and Co., New York, 1949, p. 342.

PAGE 59. "The pain and the happiness . . ." Charlotte and Howard Clinebell, *The Intimate Marriage,* Harper & Row, New York, 1970, p. 39.

PAGE 59. Sam Levenson, *Everything But Money,* Simon and Schuster, New York, 1966, p. 17.

PAGE 60. Leo Baeck, p. 122.

VII. *Overcoming the Failure of Sex Today*

PAGE 66. "Sex without commitment . . ." Debora Phillips, "Is Promiscuity Passé?" *Harper's Bazaar,* June 1982, pp. 103, 164.

PAGE 66. "in slaying. . . ." George Leonard, *The End of Sex—Erotic Love After the Sexual Revolution,* Houghton, Mifflin Co., Boston 1983, p. 10. Copy-

PAGE 66. "We need to discard . . ." ibid., p. 13.

PAGE 67. "Many therapists today . . ." Rollo May, *Love and Will*, p. 60.

PAGE 67. "Lack of will . . ." ibid., pp. 211–12.

PAGE 71. Lois Wyse, *Love Poems for the Very Married*, World Publishing Co., Cleveland, 1967, p. 29.

PAGE 71. Charlotte and Howard Clinebell, *The Intimate Marriage*, p. 31.

PAGE 72. Loren Eiseley, *The Immense Journey*, Vintage Books, New York, 1957, p. 13.

PAGE 72. *Gates of Prayer*, p. 170. The prayer alludes to Exodus 3:2 and Genesis 28:16ff. Observe also how the traditional Jewish devotions arouse one each morning to an awareness of the wonders all about. Thus in the familiar Modeh Ani we greet the day with: "I thank You, ever-living King, that You have restored my soul to me" (after the torpor of sleep). And subsequent prayers marvel at the intricacy of the human body, and at the light which God makes "to shine over the earth and all its inhabitants."

PAGE 73. Harvey Gochros, in *Human Sexuality and Social Work*, edited by H. Gochros and L. Schultz, Association Press, 1972, p. 127.

PAGE 73. "Ish . . . Ishah . . ." Talmud, Sota 17a.

PAGE 74. Ross Snyder, *Inscape*, Abingdon Press, Nashville, 1968, p. 16.

PAGE 74. Proverbs 31:16, 18–21, 25–6.

PAGE 75. "In one of the stores . . ." Midrash, Genesis Rabba 17:7.

PAGE 75. Rabbi Jose, Talmud, Shabbat 118b.

PAGE 75. Story of Beruriah, Talmud, Berachot 10a. Another cherished account tells how Beruriah used the same blend of wisdom and rabbinic skill in applying verses, to ease her husband over the shock of grief. Rabbi Meir had been away when his two sons died suddenly. When he returned, Beruriah said: "I have a question to ask of you. Early today a man came and gave me something to keep for him. Now he has come back to ask it of me. Shall I return it to him or not?" He replied: "He who has received something on deposit must surely return it to its owner." (There are many rabbinic references to such situations.) She then took him by the hand and led him to the bedroom to show him his sons. As he fell into weeping she said: "Did you not say that one must return a deposit to its owner? And does it not say: 'The Lord gave, the Lord took, blessed be the name of the Lord'?" Thus she comforted him. (Midrash to Proverbs 31:10; 54b.)

VIII. The Mystic Doctrine of Oneness

PAGE 81. "the delight which inheres . . ." Alan Watts, *Nature, Man and Woman*, Pantheon Books, a Division of Random House, New York, 1958, p. 189.

PAGE 82. George Leonard, *The End of Sex—Erotic Love after the Sexual Revolution*, Houghton, Mifflin Co., Boston, 1983, p. 214.

PAGE 82. "succeeded in establishing . . ." Gershon G. Scholem, *Zohar*, Schocken Books, New York, 1940, p. 7.

PAGE 82. Abraham Joshua Heschel, *The Earth Is the Lord's*, p. 70. Copyright 1949 by Abraham Joshua Heschel. Copyright renewed 1977 by Silvia Heschel, executrix of the estate of Abraham Joshua Heschel. Reprinted by permission of Farrar, Straus & Giroux, Inc.

PAGE 84. "the male-female design . . ." Note how Taoism, the popular religion of the Chinese, with origins attributed to the ancient Lao-tzu, describes the yin and the yang, the female and male principles of nature, which by their interaction brought forth heaven and earth, and continue to reveal their underlying processes.

PAGE 84. "The Shechina (Divine Presence) . . ." Zohar Hadash 4.50b. See also Zohar IV: Vayikra 5a.

PAGE 85. Gershon G. Scholem, *Major Trends in Jewish Mysticism*, Schocken Books, New York, 1946, p. 235.

PAGE 86. "Guard this mystery . . ." *Iggeret HaKodesh, The Holy Letter*, p. 50.

PAGE 86. "Raza de Shabta . . ." Zohar III:63b.

PAGE 87. "the interrelation of sex, God, and the Sabbath." The double significance of martial intimacy on the Sabbath, being both for the couple and for the Divine Economy, was considered by the Zohar as a manifestation of the long-held concept that "the Sabbath is a day of two portions." The original basis of the "two portions" is found in the Torah's description of the double portion of manna which was provided in the wilderness each Friday to take care both of that day and of the following when no gathering was permitted (Exodus 16:22). The Talmud connected the concept with the "additional soul" (Neshama Yetera) which elevates the Jew on the seventh day.

PAGE 87. " 'conjugal rights' . . ." Exodus 21:11. Mishna, Ketubot 5:6.

PAGE 87. "During the time. . . ." *Iggeret HaKodesh, Epistle on Holiness*, in *Kitve Ramban*, Vol. 2, ed. Chavel, Yerushalayim, 1963, pp. 335–6, translated by Zvi A. Yehuda.

PAGE 88. "The Talmud says . . ." Pesachim 49b.

PAGE 88. "I garb myself . . ." Quoted by Eugene B. Borowitz, *Choosing a Sex Ethic*, Schocken Books for B'nai B'rith Foundation, New York, 1969, p. 163.

PAGE 88. "O Lord, let there be . . ." Ibid., p. 165.

PAGE 89. Eric Fromm, *The Art of Loving*, p. 60.

Epilogue: *A Personal Validation*

PAGE 98. "Eshet Chayil . . ." and "The heart of her husband . . ." It is customary for the husband to quote from the end of the book of Proverbs (31:10 and following) as a blessing for his wife at the Sabbath table.

ABOUT THE AUTHOR

Love and youth have been the theme songs in the long and still-active career of Rabbi Alan S. Green. Having graduated from Western Reserve University, and then securing a Master's Degree in sociology, Rabbi Green was ordained at the Hebrew Union College in Cincinnati in 1934, which awarded him the Leo W. Simon Fellowship in Jewish Philosophy. He earned his Doctorate in that field after three years of graduate teaching and study there and at the Hebrew University in Jerusalem.

Four days before he was ordained, he married Frances Katz, teacher, Hebraist, and social worker, who became a close partner in his life's work. The founding of Temple Emanu El of Cleveland (1947) and its successful nurturing became the fulfillment of their careers. Celebrating his retirement thirty years later, the congregation named him Founding Rabbi. A month later Frances succumbed to cancer.

In 1979 Rabbi Green remarried. As they had shared his sorrows, his congregants now shared his joys in his marriage to Sylvia Redlick, whose outreaching spirit and wise counsel are new assets of Emanu El.

In the community Rabbi Green has labored for interfaith and interracial harmony. He has been active in the Commissions on Education and on Worship of the Reform movement and in the Central Conference of American Rabbis.

Rabbi Green's published writings cover a span of over fifty years, including regular columns in *The Synagogue* and *Liberal Judaism*, and his books *A Short History of the Jews* (with Jacob Golub) and *Return to Prayer*. His latest volume, on marriage, has brought him to speak in many communities. Each year he serves as keynote lecturer for a local workshop for young couples on "How to Stay Married."

ABOUT THE ART AND THE ARTIST

The silhouette illustrations that illuminate the manuscript are the work of Jean Tetalman, whose present endeavor is the re-creation of the folk art of Paperschnit, or paper cutting, once practiced among Jewish and other ethnic groups. In it a single piece of paper is cut out with a sharp tool to form the image. Sometimes the paper is first folded and then cut to provide a symmetry in all or part of the design.

Jean Tetalman studied at the Art Students League in New York, and at the Cleveland Institute of Art. She has emphasized Jewish themes in her work in textiles, in sculpture, and now in paper. These have been included in numerous exhibits, including invitationals. For many years she has been the Art Director of Temple Emanu El, which has been enhanced by her creation of the Torah mantels, the portable Wedding Canopy and, with Frances Green, the enamel-on-copper lobby mural of "Jerusalem of Gold." She is married to artist Jack Tetalman.